ADVENTURE ROADS
of BC's Northwest Heartland

CONTENTS

Introduction 9

1. Along the Deadman River: *Geology in Full Colour* 19
2. Nisga'a Highway: *Across the Fields of Lava* 37
3. The First Gold Rush Trail: *Along the Fraser* 55
4. Soda Creek: *A History Remembered* 77
5. Lillooet to Pemberton: *Lakes and Rivers* 91
6. Fort St. James: *An Adventure into Early History* 117
7. The Back Road to Barkerville 131
8. Heartlands of the Gitxsan: *The Totem Villages along the Skeena* 151
9. Tracking an Old Murder through the Nicola Hills 167
10. Chilcotin: *The Long and Lonely Road to the Sea* 185

Recommended Reading 212

Index 214

Gitwinksihlkw
Nass Valley Hot Springs
Nass River
Gitlaxt'aamiks
Gingolx
Nass Road
Tseax Cone Trailhead
CANADA
USA
Laxgalts'ap (Greenville)
Rosswood
Kitsumkalum Lake
113
Nisga'a Highway
Terrace
Prince Rupert
16
Skeena River
37
Gitanyow
Gitwangak
Gitsegukla
Battle Hill Historic Site
Skeena
Kispiox (Anspayaxw)
Hazelton
'Ksan
Tse-kya
Bulkley Canyon
Witset (Moricetown)
Bulkley River
Smithers
Houston
N
50 km

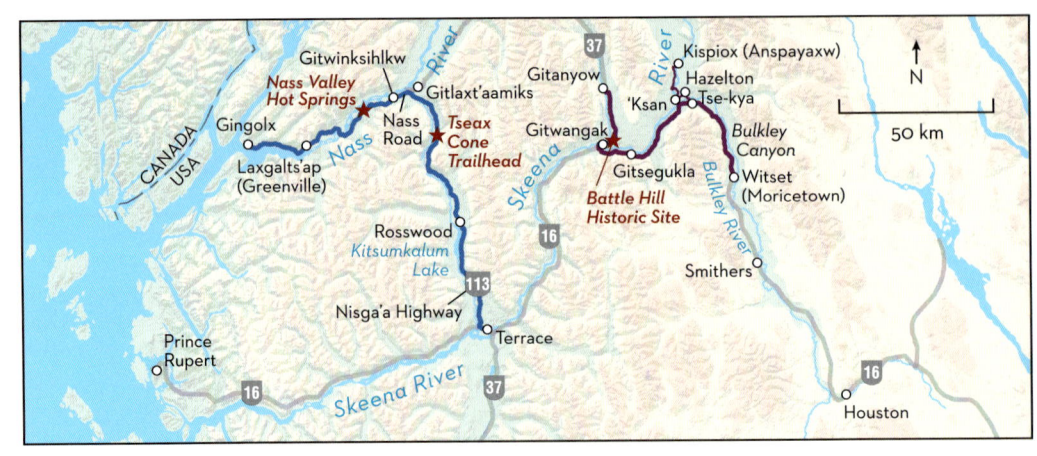

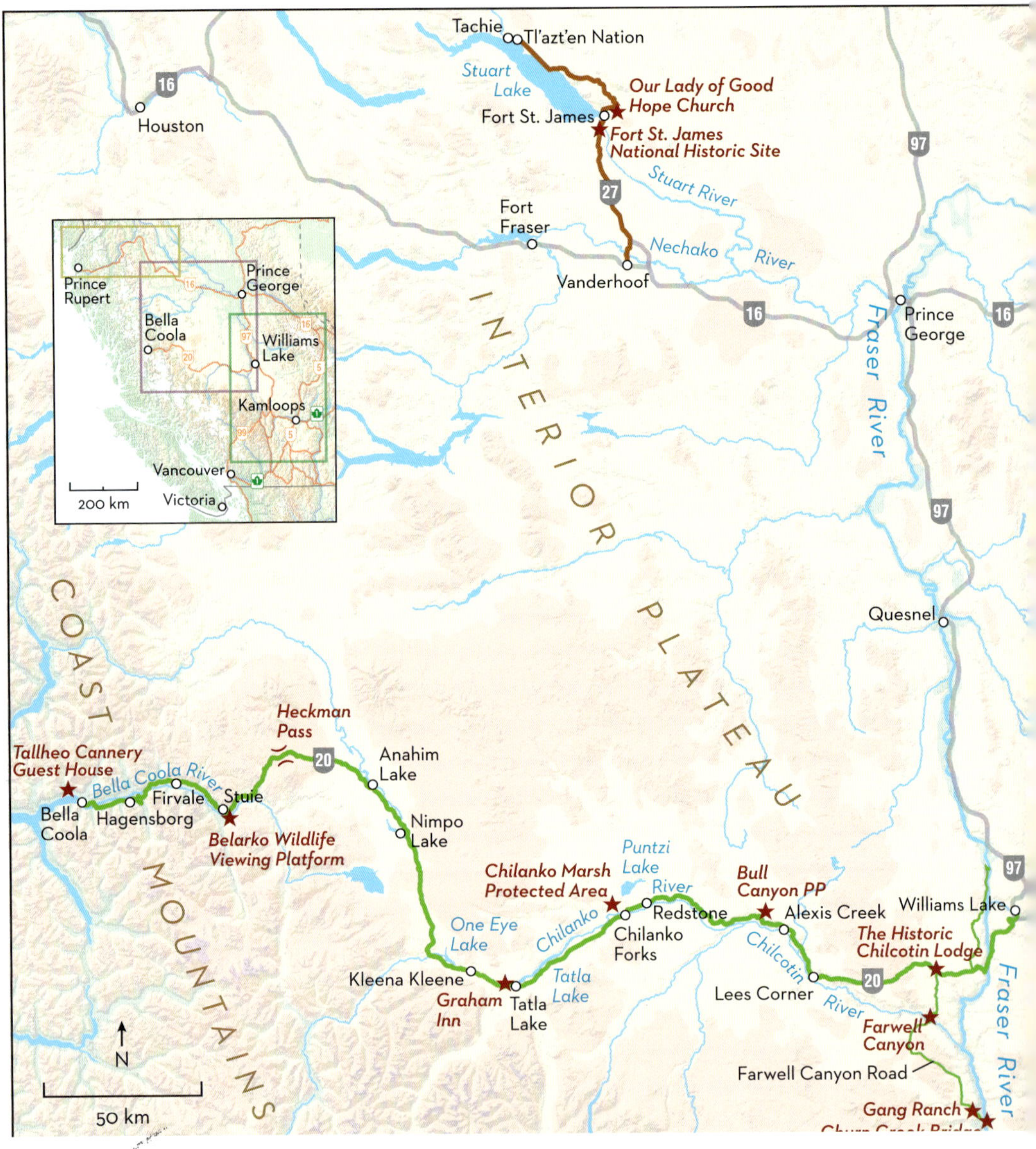

Tachie
Tl'azt'en Nation
Stuart Lake
Our Lady of Good Hope Church
Fort St. James
Fort St. James National Historic Site
Stuart River
27
Fort Fraser
Nechako River
Vanderhoof
16
Houston
97
Prince George
Fraser River
INTERIOR PLATEAU
Prince Rupert
Prince George
Bella Coola
Williams Lake
Kamloops
Vancouver
Victoria
200 km
Quesnel
COAST MOUNTAINS
Heckman Pass
20
Tallheo Cannery Guest House
Bella Coola River
Bella Coola
Hagensborg
Firvale
Stuie
Belarko Wildlife Viewing Platform
Anahim Lake
Nimpo Lake
Puntzi Lake
Chilanko Marsh Protected Area
Bull Canyon PP
One Eye Lake
Chilanko River
Redstone
Alexis Creek
Williams Lake
Chilanko Forks
The Historic Chilcotin Lodge
Chilcotin River
Kleena Kleene
Graham Inn
Tatla Lake
Lees Corner
Farwell Canyon
Farwell Canyon Road
Gang Ranch
N
50 km

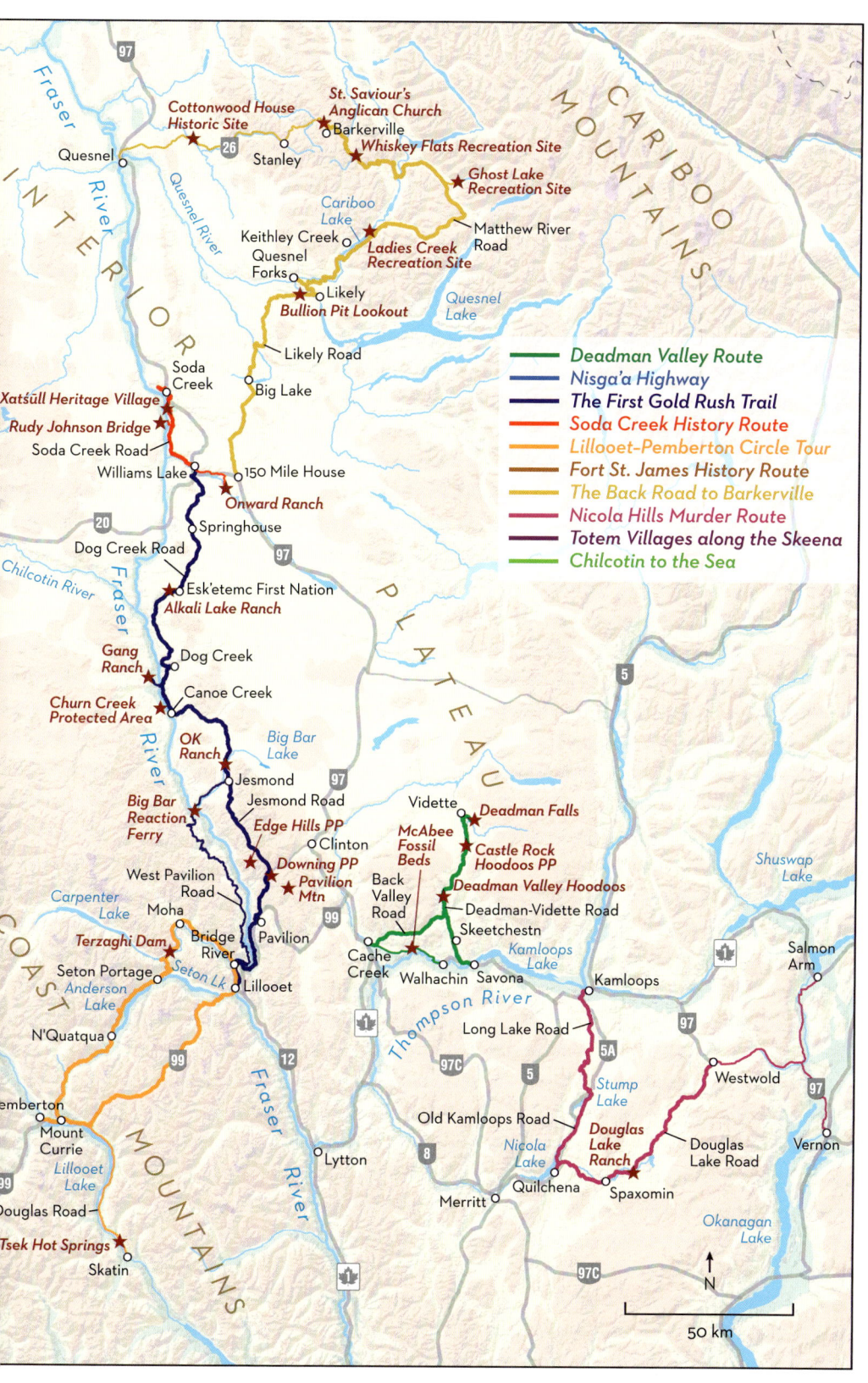

INTRODUCTION

The *Oxford English Dictionary* defines adventure as both a noun—"daring enterprise"—and a verb—"to incur risk." *Roget's Super Thesaurus*, far easier to use than his original, suggests "escapade" as a synonym for adventure. Can it be used to describe a road?

I think so. Roads can certainly *lead* to an escapade, not always of the visceral kind, but of the mind and the emotions. Entwined with the history of the land and the stories of the people who have lived here through the decades, the centuries, adventure roads are like books: with every turn of the page or curve in the road they reveal something new and wonderful.

The journeys in this book traverse only a part of the huge province of British Columbia. They are found in what could be described as the northwestern heartland, stretching north from Merritt to Barkerville, west from Kamloops all the way to Bella Coola, then northwest from Prince George to the ocean. BC's major highways provide links to these remarkable escapades.

Most of the roads in this book were described in my *Country Roads of British Columbia: Exploring the Interior*, first published in 2008 and now out of print. It was interesting to see, in 2021, just how much has changed—and also how very much of the land remains as it was then.

OPPOSITE A street in the ghost town of Quesnelle Forks.

A cowboy at work, gently guiding a string of Herefords across the grasslands. A scene typical of the Cariboo-Chilcotin.

BC is a hard land, a huge land, divided by deeply chiselled mountain ranges, riven by fierce rivers and long lakes, and cloaked in thick forests, with a climate that ranges from near arctic to desert. In this fractured topography extreme weather conditions create havoc—avalanches, rockfalls, landslides, floods, and also drought, high winds, and forest fires. In the summer of 2021, whole villages were almost destroyed by flood or fire, roads and bridges were washed away or blocked by mudslides, a sudden acceleration of disaster that is blamed on global warming.

An understanding of the province's landforms is an adventure for the mind. The strong north-south trend of the province's major features can be explained, in part and very simply, by the way the land was formed—in bits and pieces, like a patchwork quilt. Strings of volcanic islands (geologists call them terranes), formed far out in the Pacific Ocean, drifted eastward, slowly but inexorably toward the granite bones of ancestral North America. On impact, these island continents distorted the land they joined, pushing up great mountain ranges. The seams between each new terrane became valleys, which later filled with ice, rivers, and lakes. Over the millennia, volcanic

The Skeetchestn graveyard at Deadman Valley.

activity, glaciers, and erosion were catalysts for more change, but the different terranes can usually still be singled out and recognized.

The valley seams of BC's fractured landscapes house most of today's highways, homesteads, ranches, villages, towns, and cities, all of which can trace their beginnings to the gold rush of the Victorian and Edwardian eras, the heyday of British colonial expansionism and pride—and missionary zeal. But we must recognize and acknowledge the truth: that all this marvellous land, now indelibly stamped with nearly two hundred years of European civilization, was taken from its original inhabitants whose own beliefs and ways of life and even languages were harshly repressed, their lives seen as having little value. It is a wonder that the Indigenous peoples are still here, in all their spiritual strength. We who marched into their ancient lands must sincerely apologize for past wrongs and work to ensure full recognition of their rights. As we travel through their sacred world of myths and legends and creativity, we can only treasure the rich history and beauty they bring to the world.

FOLLOWING SPREAD The Gang Ranch sprawls across river benchland, looking across the deep valley of the Fraser River to the hills above.

ABOVE Fiery crags along the Deadman River Valley.

OPPOSITE The Bulkley River, north of Smithers, roars through a tight rock canyon, a traditional hot spot for Indigenous fishermen.

NOTE You'll notice that some places on the routes in this book have two names. The newer ones, given by the first settlers, are likely to be marked on the road maps but many of the signs along the way now also display the original First Nations names. Wherever possible, I provide both names and have used Nation websites for the correct spellings.

The map in this book is for general reference only. If you set out on a road trip, be sure you also have a good British Columbia road map with you. I also like to have on hand books in the Backroad Mapbooks series. They show all the roads, as well as topography and information on parks, trails, and recreational possibilities. These spiral-bound books are widely available and can also be ordered online at backroadmapbooks.com. And there is, of course, Google Maps, but be aware that there is no internet connection on many stretches of road.

FOLLOWING SPREAD A ghost ranch in the upper Deadman Valley.

1. ALONG THE DEADMAN RIVER
GEOLOGY IN FULL COLOUR

British Columbia's South Thompson River, east of Kamloops, runs through some of the driest land in Canada: parched craggy hillsides peppered with sagebrush and cactus, knapweed, thistles—and rattlesnakes. In summer, the land is hot, dusty, and drab. In the late nineteenth century, a group of British immigrants came up with a scheme to turn this desert into apple orchards. Ensconced in the small settlement of Walhachin, beside the river, they brought in irrigation water, not up from the Thompson—at the time there were no suitable pumps—but by gravity feed along huge lengths of wooden troughs and ditches from lakes at the north end of the Deadman Valley, about sixty kilometres distant.

The road along the Deadman River leads north into an amazing landscape where the Walhachin story began. It leaves behind the dry dust of Thompson River benches and travels deep into the heart of ancient earth history, straddling the seam between two of the separate land masses that fused into what is now British Columbia. Even to a novice geologist, the eastern and western edges of the flamboyant Deadman Valley appear completely different. On the west side,

OPPOSITE These hoodoos are perhaps the most interesting of all the volcanic formations, but one needs binoculars to see them.

the relatively flat and forested Interior Plateau rises high at the top of sheer basaltic columns, the exposed edge of a thick layer of lava that covers ancient bedrock formed around 5 million years ago during the Miocene-Pliocene era. To the east, deeply fractured and fissured, the land is younger, formed during the Holocene-Pleistocene era, about 1.6 million years ago. Here the slopes are walled with strange, fire-coloured rock formations, mostly formed from solidified volcanic ash. It is an exciting journey, both aesthetically and geologically, following the river from desert through ranchland and forests, to a string of little lakes, an abandoned gold mine, and an astounding sixty-metre-high waterfall.

At Savona, Highway 1 bridges the Thompson River at the western end of Kamloops Lake and continues west to cross the Deadman River just upstream of its confluence delta. Deadman is a fitting name: it was along the river banks here that a fur trader by the name of Pierre Charette, a clerk at the North West Company's Fort Kamloops, was knifed to death in 1817.

Up the hill from the bridge, the Deadman adventure road, signposted Deadman/Vidette, escapes the highway and leads first to the Indigenous village of Skeetchestn. This is a historic spot. Secwepemc peoples from as far away as Pavilion and Kamloops once gathered here to participate in traditional ceremonies and harvest trout from the river. The once bountiful fishery is now in decline, and as part of an ongoing restoration project, the Skeetchestn People operate a hatchery nearby. Historic St. Mary's Church, built in the village in 1910 on the site of an earlier log structure, has been well looked after, renovated, and is still in use.

The colourful lesson in earth history is all on the east side of the valley road. At Criss Creek, which enters the Deadman from the northeast about six kilometres beyond the village, spectacular serrated cliffs in hues of deep orange-red provide a dramatic contrast to

OPPOSITE St. Mary's Church, Skeetchestn.

FOLLOWING SPREAD Traces of the old wooden flume that brought water down the valley and across the Thompson River to the ill-fated community of Walhachin.

OPPOSITE Split Rocks, an apt name for such fissured volcanic attractions.

ABOVE Green fields of a valley ranch, overlooked by rainbow rocks.

the green of adjacent irrigated ranch fields. You'll find parking beside the creek bridge in the shade of cottonwood trees, a good place to study the geology. Beyond, across another bridge, a short leafy track invites a stroll along the river's edge across from other incredible rock formations, seventy metres high and resplendent in brilliant shades of red, dark purple, and grey-green. The road climbs higher, providing a grandstand view of these spectacular bluffs. Known locally and on some maps as Split Rocks, they are mostly of igneous origin and interlayered with sedimentary deposits, which accounts for the differential weathering—and the contorted folds, caves, and vertical cracks. A side road heading west just opposite the rocks provides an optional return route to Highway 1 near Cache Creek.

The valley ranchlands continue, still bordered along their eastern side by volcanic outcrops. Keep watch higher up on the valley slopes for formations of a different nature: five eroded hoodoos of sand and clay, each about ten to twelve metres tall, topped with caps of harder rock. Only four are visible from the road (the fifth is tucked into the gully) and they are far away, but they stand out clearly, pale yellow above the

Eroded rocks form pinnacles at Criss Creek.

fiery colours of billowing volcanic formations. Binoculars are useful here. At present, there is no public access to these formations.

Past the hoodoos, the valley becomes tighter, the river closer, the hillsides more forested. Keep an eye out for the Circle W Ranch: the pretty white bungalow with its shady veranda was moved here from Walhachin when the town declined. (See page 34.) About twenty-five kilometres from the highway, the road bridges the Deadman River as it hurtles through a tight rock canyon, and starts into the forests. Now the valley is narrow, almost filled with a string of six lakes: Mowich (Shuswap for "deer"); Snohoosh, site of the 1910 Walhachin dam; Skookum, Deadman, Outpost, and Vidette, all stocked with rainbow and kokanee trout.

Patterns in colours and shapes.

The geology lesson continues at the Castle Rock Hoodoos Provincial Park, beside the road at Skookum Lake. Rising sixty metres above the road, the eroded yellow sandstone cliffs with their crenellated tops do indeed look like a castle. The park was set up in 1997 to protect these fragile cliffs and no foot traffic is allowed: you can see everything right from the road. This tiny provincial park offers no facilities, but there are forestry campsites at three of the lakes: Deadman, Outpost, and Vidette.

The Deadman River rises on the high Cariboo Plateau, east of the valley, and rushes steeply down into Vidette Lake. The road bridges the river and follows the shoreline of the lake to the end of the valley, about fifty kilometres from Highway 1. This lake was the halfway point on one of the Hudson's Bay brigade trails between Fort Kamloops on the Thompson River and Fort Alexandria on the Fraser, and there was a small trading post here.

In 1931, geologists found veins of gold-bearing quartz on the hillside above the lake and a large mining operation was begun, both above ground and in eight kilometres of tunnels. Vidette Mine became one of the richest producers of gold in the 1930s, and a work

An old log cabin on the way to the lakes.

camp and later a small village were established near the head of the lake. Miners were paid 50 cents an hour and were charged $1.50 a day for board and lodging in the company camp. To bring men and supplies in and gold out, more than thirty-five kilometres of road along the lakes were bulldozed—the road you have been travelling. Mining continued at full steam for more than six years and then, as the rich gold content petered out and the Second World War began, activity fizzled out. Most of the buildings have gone, but the mine workings are still there—if you know where to look. One of the mine tunnels can be seen beside the road at the Vidette Lake campsite. It doesn't look very big. It must have been a tight squeeze to get in and out.

At the end of the lake, a small resort, with a lodge and several cabins, one of them constructed from timbers from the old HBC post, was closed in the summer of 2021 and looked as if it had been closed for several years. Beyond the lodge gates, the road climbs very steeply via a series of switchback up into the open forests of the plateau, where it meets the river again. On the top there is a clearing in the aspens drained by creeks in three different directions. A visiting Tibetan monk once decided that this was the Centre of the Universe. Onsite meditations seemingly confirmed this, and the place is now occasionally visited by mystics from around the world. Whether you find the site mystical or not, the high, flowery meadow has a fine view south over the lake—and this is magic enough for me.

Deadman Road continues through the high forest, and about six kilometres beyond Vidette Lake is Deadman Falls Recreation Site. You can hear the wild rush of the water as you approach but you might miss the trail that leads you to the falls. Watch for red-painted "Falls" signs on the trunks of two trees. In spring and early summer, the thunder of the water as it chutes down the sixty-metre-high cliff can be deafening, and the spray is flung so high there are rainbows in the river at its base. This is a wild waterfall: there are no guardrails, and it's a huge drop down the cliffs into the boiling eddy. Tread carefully. With a wide-angle lens, you should be able to photograph the falls, top to bottom, from sky to magical rainbows.

The return route is simply retracing the way you came, but the geological treasures along the valley are well worth a second look, as the shifting sun reveals new facets of their personality. At Split Rocks, take the alternative route back to Highway 1. A side road, well signposted, it follows Charette Creek (named after the murdered fur trader) across a low divide then picks up Cache Creek (the actual creek) into Pass Valley. Open pine woodlands and three small lakes encourage slow driving. There are wildflowers and birds—look for loons, sandpipers, grebes, kingfishers, warblers, and swallows—and even a colony of bats. But the scenery changes. Soon the road is back into the desert scrub and sagebrush that line Highway 1. There is another cliff of eroded red rocks near the highway, but if you are tempted to explore, watch your step: they are named Rattlesnake Rocks for good reason.

The adventure road ends just east of Cache Creek, but for those

FOLLOWING SPREAD The road up the Deadman Valley follows a string of lakes. This last one is Vidette, once the site of a gold mine.

ABOVE Above the valley, hand-painted signs lead through the forest to Deadman Falls.

LEFT Sun and water create shifting rainbows above the pool.

OPPOSITE A fitting climax to this adventure: Deadman Falls drops sixty metres into a large pool.

in search of more geology, the McAbee Fossil Beds Heritage Site, a short distance east, will satisfy. An ancient lake bed here preserves a spectacular trove of fossilized plants and insects from the Eocene epoch, around 40 million to 50 million years ago. The site, on the Bonaparte First Nations Reserve, is currently fenced and in 2021 was closed to the public while plans were being made for trails and the building of an interpretive centre.

SIDE TRIP

WALHACHIN: LOST DREAMS

For a dip into more recent history, drive east on Highway 1 and watch for the signpost to Walhachin, the settlement whose orchards were once fed by water from Deadman Valley lakes. The little town is still there, on the south side of the Thompson River. You can reach it by crossing a one-lane bridge burdened by a huge osprey nest on the overhead girders. Almost deserted when the men left to fight in the First World War, Walhachin is such an attractive place that people seem to be moving back in, though there are no facilities, not even a store or picnic site. Residents have placed several park benches along the river's edge, a good place to stop and take in the view. When the village was established back in the early 1900s, there were several streets of houses on the river bench, a large hotel (opened with much fanfare by Prime Minister Wilfrid Laurier), and a village hall with a floating dance floor. Homes were mostly low-slung Colonial bungalows, with wide wraparound verandas, and some of these remain. Others were moved when the town virtually closed. If you look carefully, you can still find them in places such as Kamloops, Cache Creek, and even the Deadman Valley.

The hotel is long gone, but the hall, remodelled as the Walhachin Soldiers Memorial Hall, is still there, complete with its well-sprung dance floor, and for a while residents maintained a small museum there, although it is now closed. Still, the hall helps visitors to remember that when the First World War broke out in August 1914, all but one of the resident single men signed up to form the Walhachin Squadron of the 31st Regiment, The British Columbia Horse, and left for England. Most of the soldiers returned, but very few chose to stay. By then flumes were broken and the apple trees dead of thirst. It was the wrong place for orchards: it is hot in summer and very cold in winter, and on average the South Thompson country receives less than twenty centimetres of rain a year.

Today, the surrounding hills are mostly cattle range, and there are several ranches in the area. But Walhachin, unexpectedly, has a rabbit ranch, where many different breeds are raised and shipped around the world. Don't expect to find Peter Rabbits hopping around, though. They are all in airy cages.

Thompson Bridge.

2. NISG̲A'A HIGHWAY
ACROSS THE FIELDS OF LAVA

Imagine a BC landscape after the ravages of a violent volcanic eruption. The trees and vegetation are gone, the whole valley is smothered under a carpet of rumpled hardened lava, rock so deep it has buried two whole villages and killed thousands of people. Creeks are dammed and the great Nass River itself (its Nisga'a name is K'alii-askim Lisims) is pushed aside. The Nass Valley, centre of the Nisga'a world, is almost dead space.

This adventure road, one of BC's truly great journeys, leads through a strange volcanic landscape—after almost 250 years it has changed very little—then follows the Nass River out to the sea, to the edge of the Great Bear Rainforest. There is far more than geological excitement here. It is also a cultural excursion into the land of the Nisga'a, people who were strong enough to remain in their injured valley, rebuilding their villages, preserving their stories, their ceremonies, their language, and honouring their ancestors. The Nisga'a were also determined enough to challenge governments successfully for their land rights and titles. Today, Highway 152 from the Skeena to the Nass has been designated Highway 113, the number of years it took for Nisga'a land claims to be accepted. Culture and geology—an adventurous combination.

OPPOSITE Mist rises like smoke from the lava beds.

New Aiyansh Community Centre.

The journey begins just west of the town of Terrace, where Highway 113 leads north into the heart of Nisga'a territory. The only pioneer settlement of note along the first part of the road, just north of long Kitsumkalum Lake, is Rosswood, which has an old general store. Forty kilometres north of Terrace, it's an interesting community. Reached only by boat along the lake until 1954 when the highway came through, it lived without hydro until 1999 and phone service until 2001. It is known for its unique forty-year-old roadside "Magic Tree," which delivers clear creek water from a spigot inserted in its trunk.

Farther north, the bridge across Cedar Creek marks a geological divide down into the Nass Valley by way of Sand Lake and the Tseax River. The first sign of the volcano's action is found at Lava Lake, a narrow ten-kilometre-long finger that fills the valley floor. Formed when lava dammed the Tseax River, the lake and its surrounds are now part of Nisga'a Memorial Lava Beds Provincial Park, which extends all the way to the Nass and beyond. The lake has an

Lava Lake: clear and green.

otherworldly aspect: rimmed by sheets of broken, moss-covered lava, its colour is a startling milky green, the reflections very clear. Its Nisga'a name is Sii T'axl, or "new lake." A picnic site at its northern end has a canoe-launching ramp.

The Tseax River is still trying to find its way through the changed landscape. Sometimes it disappears beneath the honeycombed lava, emerging to form deep green pools that flood the forest, and several pretty waterfalls tumble into it. The trail at Crater Creek, now partly covered by lava flow (the creek's original name, Lax Mihl, means "on top of fire"), is a good place for a short walk. Go carefully, though: the lava is sharp and uncomfortable. The Tseax Cone, the volcanic source, is high above the valley and can only be reached by a steep hike led by a park guide. Check at the Park Visitor Centre farther down the valley, which offers a self-directed guide to all the points of interest. The centre is housed in a replica of a Nisga'a longhouse, its facade painted with clan emblems. The park campsite is adjacent.

The Longhouse replica at the Lava Beds Park Visitor Centre.

Nothing can prepare you for the first astounding sight of the volcanic destruction: the whole valley has been flattened, encased in a huge, shell of rumpled lava. The ground is barren, although mosses and lichens are doing their best to bring a little softness and colour, and a few cracks and crevices provide fragile toeholds for skimpy trees and shrubs. Above it all, in great contrast, snowy mountains rise high on both sides of the valley, their forests a deep and luscious green. On the ground, morning mists hover above the lava fields like smoke.

Park signs describe the geological features through this eerie landscape, and short trails lead to some of them. There are two types of lava—smooth and wrinkled, lava tubes, like huge drainpipes, and tree moulds bearing the imprints of long-lost forest giants.

The destructive volcanic eruption, still remembered in the oral history of the Nisga'a, is explained in an old story passed down through the generations. Many years ago, young boys playing beside the river caught some salmon and poked lighted sticks into their backs. They put the fish back into the water and laughed to see them writhe in agony, trying to swim away.

A close-up of the circular doorway.

Retribution came swiftly: The mountains roared and a great pillar of smoke and fire appeared. The people watched in terror as a river of burning molten rock surged relentlessly down into the valley. Many were overcome by deadly fumes; others fled as best they could, or tried to hide in earth cellars. When the violent episode was over, the Nisga'a world had changed forever. Their whole valley and two of their villages were buried under a thick blanket of solidified lava, and more than two thousand people were dead.

A written report of the event has also survived. In 1775, sailors on the Spanish ship *Sonora*, under the command of explorer Juan Francisco de la Bodega y Quadra, witnessed the eruption from the mouth of the Nass River. The expedition chronicler described great heat and flames shooting up from four or five mouths of a volcano and fires so bright they lit up the night.

Scientific radiometric dating confirms two eruptions in the Nass Valley, approximately 650 and 250 years ago, and offers evidence of other older flows. The culprit volcano, pinpointed today by the cinder cone, erupted violently, spewing lava downhill for

Totem near Gitwinksihlkw Bridge.

five kilometres, where it piled up, damming the Tseax River and spilling over to flow another twenty-two kilometres down and across the Nass Valley. More than thirty-eight square kilometres of fertile coastal forest was gone, and in its place lay a wasteland of solidified lava. It was Canada's worst known geophysical disaster.

At an intersection almost one hundred kilometres from Highway 16, the Nisga'a Highway turns east, away from the lava fields, for access to the village once known as New Aiyansh. It's now Gitlaxt'aamiks, the name of the previous riverside settlement, which suffered many devastating floods. The original site was abandoned and a new village built higher up the mountain in 1974. As the largest of the four villages, it is the seat of the Nisga'a government, and the design of its parliament building, an expanded traditional longhouse, honours tribal culture and heritage. There are totems inside and out, displays of local carvings, and a public gallery in conical form, emulates the shape of Tseax Peak—all very symbolic. Nisga'a totems and designs are everywhere in the village: the large community hall and the school are well worth seeking out for their striking artwork.

The Nisga'a Highway itself continues east for about fifty unpaved kilometres all the way to Cranberry Junction, where it joins Highway 37 on its way to Yukon. Back at the intersection, Nass Road continues our journey to the sea. The stark lava plain spreads

TOP Old Gitwinksihlkw Bridge.

BOTTOM Smothered valley, lost villages.

NISG̱A'A HIGHWAY: ACROSS THE FIELDS OF LAVA

The Nisga'a Museum, a towering architectural masterpiece of symbolic design.

throughout the valley, and park signs indicate prominent features. One is a memorial plaque to mourn the people of the lost villages. A sign here urges visitors not to move the lava rocks since they "are the gravestones of our ancestors."

Turn right (north) after a few kilometres to visit Gitwinksihlkw, or "people of the lizards," another of the Nisga'a villages on the Nass River. Before the volcano erupted, the village site was in a damp place where salamanders were common. They too disappeared under the lava. At the entrance to the village, a modern bridge across

ABOVE Inside the museum, a replica of a traditional longhouse, with its stunning entrance carving, opens onto a theatrical display of once-lost spirit masks and regalia, recently repatriated. Photos by Gary Fiegehen, courtesy of the Nisga'a Lisims Government.

FOLLOWING SPREAD Crows keep watch along the estuary shore.

A fishboat hauled up for repairs near Laxgalts'ap is a reminder that fishing has always been a mainstay for the Nisga'a People.

the Nass is flanked by new totem poles depicting the four Nisga'a clans, Wolf, Eagle, Raven, and Killer Whale. Before the road and the bridge were built in 1995, a skinny footbridge suspended high above the river provided the only land access. Villagers had to boat downriver to Gingolx (Kincolith) to pick up supplies brought in by steamer from Prince Rupert.

The old suspension bridge, constructed in 1969, the last of many similar structures built here, was left in place, and it's worth a wobbly walk across it. High on the swaying planks above the Nass, you can see and feel the river's raw power and look across the sea of lava to the mountains. There are fish-counting wheels for salmon near here, and old grave markers in the long grass beside the bridge. The very tall pole at the community centre, raised in 1992, was the first carved in the village in more than a century.

Return across the Nass to the main road and continue west along the valley, first through the lava field and then into coastal forest. Hot springs beside the road, open to all, might tempt you to linger. They are well signed, and wood decks provide easy access to the natural pool. The Nisga'a believe this to be the home of a mighty naxnok, or spirit, and that the sulphurous smell of the water is his breath.

About twenty kilometres from Gitwinksihlkw, where the road forks, a one-way bridge, one of several on the route, leads across the Nass, a river now very much wider and less braided as it approaches its estuary. Gulls wheel and call over the water. Notice the air. If you stop and sniff, surely there's the salt tang of the sea?

The village of Greenville, about ten kilometres along the road, was named for Methodist missionary Alfred Green, who arrived here in 1877 and was tasked with persuading the villagers to abandon their old beliefs. Today, the community is called Laxgalts'ap, which means "village on village," because it is on the same site as the many others that came before it. Beside the tidal waters of Fishery Bay, where the Ishkheenickh River flows into the Nass, the village has always been a multicultural fishing ground. Visiting Tsimshian and Gitxsan were welcome to fish here, side by side with the Nisga'a.

The highlight of a visit here is the Nisga'a Museum, just a short distance west of the village. Its modern architecture alone is astonishing: it is five storeys tall, to accommodate the height of the totem pole that forms the corner point of its angled, all-glass front. A bold choice, this see-through wall brings the mountain scenery right into the lofty entrance hall. And here, a building within a building (perhaps a play on the meaning of Laxgalts'ap itself) takes the modern world right back into the rich spiritual past of the Nisga'a. Flying out from above the circular doorway of a traditional longhouse, a huge, dramatic carving captures the powerful supernatural being Txseemsim transmuted into his favourite form, the trickster, Raven. His beak, far too short for any earthly raven, protrudes like a canopy. This amazing sculpture is based on a watercolour of a house front in the old village of Lax Anhlo'o, painted in 1868 by Pym Nevins Compton, an Englishman who joined the HBC as a clerk in 1858. One of the first tourist-artists to visit the area, he painted this view during an excursion into the Nass Valley, and his work shows village children scrambling around the sculpture. This is why, if you look up into the great beak, you can see beautifully carved children at play. The

Gingolx church tower above the fireweed.

sculpture was made by a dedicated team of carvers: George McKay, Calvin McNeil, Gerald Robinson, and Albert Stephens Jr., under the technical guidance of Mel Leeson.

If this great dramatic work of art does not overwhelm you, then wait. When the red button blanket across the house doorway is drawn back, like a theatre curtain, it reveals the Ancestors' Collection on display on the stage behind. No, "display" is too poor a word. All the once-lost naxnok or spirit masks, headdresses, and regalia are worn by manikins who pose in different positions. Some stare right at you, and the lighting and reflections seem to bring them to life, another transformation. Set against a painted backdrop of mountains, this theatrical stage will surely haunt you.

Other cultural artifacts are displayed more conservatively—but just as dramatically—behind the main stage. More than three hundred recovered items are rehoused here, most of them repatriated from the Royal BC Museum in Victoria and the Canadian Museum of History in Ottawa. The price of admission includes a tour given by a local guide who will lead you deeper into the world of the Nisga'a naxnok and might share some of the old stories.

Boat Harbour pier, Gingolx.

In the village of Laxgalts'ap itself there's a carving shed (visitors welcome) beside the river, and fishing boats are tied up nearby. The big, red St. Andrew's Church is very new, built in 1990 to replace its predecessor, which burned in 1962. A troupe of traditional Nisga'a dancers are based in the village and perhaps by 2022 they will be allowed to perform again.

Around the bend in the river at Black Point, the road runs right along the edge of the Nass estuary, which stretches wide as the opposite shore recedes, melting into a beautiful backdrop of misty mountains. Suddenly it's a maritime landscape, waves washing onto sand flats and pebble beaches heaped with seaweed and driftwood. Eagles and great flocks of gulls feed in the eelgrass and wheel overhead. This is a totally different country, fiords and forests and the surge of the sea, a dramatic contrast to the strange, barren land of lava. Eulachon still come into the river to spawn in huge numbers in February and March and are caught, dried, and traded, just as they have always been. The little fish bring an added attraction for visitors, as predators—gulls, eagles, seals, and even killer whales—come to feast on them.

The beautiful twenty-eight-kilometre drive south from Laxgalts'ap is fringed by cliffs and open to the southwestern sky. It winds past Mill Bay and Fort Point to the protected shores of Portland Inlet and the end of the road: the village of Kincolith, an Anglicized version of its original name, Gingolx, or "place of skulls." The name refers to the ancient practice of posting skulls on sticks at the river mouth to scare strangers away from the rich fishing grounds, but today, visitors are welcome here. The small fishing port (population five hundred) was until recently known for its Crabfest, a two-day musical event in July that drew performers and visitors from afar to feast not only on musical offerings but also on local crab, salmon, and halibut. Today, Crabfest is no more, but there are still excellent small fish restaurants here, including one called "U" See Food "U" Eat It!

In 1867, Robert Tomlinson, an Anglican medical missionary, floated downriver by raft and started a Protestant mission here. The village still has an impressive church. Christ Church is a huge white building with flying buttresses and Gothic windows, a very tall pinnacled steeple, and a shorter tower. Built in 1900, to replace earlier versions, it was remodelled in 1961.

With its tidy grid of streets, foreshore promenade, and wooden boardwalk out to the village dock, Gingolx still feels a bit like the English seaside village that Tomlinson tried to establish here, but the Nisga'a presence is everywhere and very strong. Explore the village, watch the eagles (there's a viewing telescope on the promenade), eat some fish and chips, then drive west through town across the long bridge over the Gingolx River mouth and follow Fisherman's Road along the shore to the harbour to look at the boats and enjoy the fresh sea winds—a restful place to end the journey.

The drive from Terrace to Gingolx, with all the many things to see and do, could easily take a full day. Check out overnight accommodations or campgrounds before you start. And after breakfast, you have another whole day to see it all again and visit the places you missed.

OPPOSITE Thimbleberries in bloom beside a rushing creek.

3. THE FIRST GOLD RUSH TRAIL
ALONG THE FRASER

Like gold rushes everywhere, the one that catapulted the infant colony of British Columbia into world headlines provoked a kind of madness. As soon as word leaked out, men left their jobs and families and made long, difficult journeys to reach the land of possibilities, where a grubstake and a gold pan might be all they needed for instant wealth. It was the great lottery of the Victorian era. Men, most of them greenhorns, arrived in huge numbers at the small, staid colonial outpost of Victoria—where they learned just how far away the goldfields were. But nobody told them of the appalling conditions along the trail. After a relatively easy trek alongside the Fraser and its sagebrush benches, ahead of them lay trackless mountains and raging rivers, thick forests and swamps, unbearably cold winters and sweaty summers, plagued by flies and mosquitoes. But they pushed on, aided by the First Nations people, whose traditional trails they relied on for much of the way, up the great river named for explorer Simon Fraser, and into the depths of the Cariboo Mountains. And here, a few of them—very few—made their fortune.

OPPOSITE The river trail winds sinuously through the hillsides above the Fraser.

OPPOSITE Holy Trinity Church at Pavilion, where the trail takes a high route over the mountain and back to the Fraser.

ABOVE The original Mountain House roadhouse, established in 1870, was renamed Jesmond, a less common post office name.

As quickly as it could, the colonial government scratched out rough roads and supply routes, most of them now today's highways. But some of the original trails remain as footpaths or narrow, unpaved roads where, if you stop long enough to feel the vibrations of history, the hectic days of the gold rush, 160 years away, can seem like yesterday.

The earliest road to the Cariboo gold, known as the River Trail, is perhaps the most adventurous of the gold-rush routes. It follows the Fraser River from Lillooet to Williams Lake—but not by the highway route. North from Pavilion the road is mostly unpaved, possibly closed in winter, likely muddy in spring, subject to landslides and washouts and certainly dusty in deep summer. But driving through the hills and across the high sagebrush shoulders of the Fraser will engulf you in a heady mix of landscape and history. Barkerville, the resurrected capital of the Cariboo camps, might well be the final

ABOVE Founded in 1859 by Joseph Haller, today's OK Ranch is the oldest along the route.

OPPOSITE The trail winds down here to the Churn Creek Bridge.

destination for today's travellers—as it was during the gold rush—but the journey there can be just as memorable.

Lillooet sits at the confluence of the Fraser River and boiling Cayoosh Creek, the centre of an ancient Indigenous settlement. An old town, it stretches long and thin on a high river bench, and in summer it is one of the hottest spots in the province. It was also a hot spot in the early days of the gold rush, when the two main gold-rush trails from the coast converged here. By 1860, with its main street peppered with thirteen saloons, it sported a shifting population of sixteen thousand. The town became Mile "0" on the Cariboo Trail, a designation that stayed even when Lillooet was later bypassed by the wagon road from Lytton.

The cairn marking Mile "0" sits on Lillooet's Main Street, opposite the museum housed in the former Anglican church. The street leads downhill to the Fraser River, where the original ferry crossing was replaced by a narrow suspension bridge, for years the town's only highway access. This was replaced in turn by the modern Bridge of the 23 Camels, at the other end of town. (This name immortalizes the camels used for a time as pack animals along the Cariboo Trail.) The suspension bridge, kept open for pedestrians, is right on the miners' original route north. Engineers stop to study its construction details, all wires

Another view of the winding road.

and bolts, and nature lovers like to visit at dusk, when clouds of bats, housed in special habitation boxes under the bridge deck, fly out.

This adventure road starts at the Highway 99 end of the Bridge of the 23 Camels and heads north past the site of the old Hudson's Bay Company (HBC) Fort Berens, home of the area's first winery. The highway is narrow and twisting, tracking the Fraser's east bank past the meadows of Fountain, a gold-rush watering hole at the site of a natural spring. The Indigenous village of Fountain (Xaxl'ip) moved up onto the bench above the road to escape the rowdy wagon-road traffic. There's a fine little church and a huge graveyard here.

Farther north is the settlement of Pavilion. For years, the general store here, built in 1930 on the site of a gold-rush stopping house, was as popular a rest stop for motorists as it had been for early wagon drivers. Shaded by a deep veranda, its garden full of flowers, including a wonderful yellow climbing rose, it kept going

The river canyon is steep, and views of the river are rare.

for half a century until one night it burned down, leaving only its tall brick chimney and a single rose bush as evidence of its existence.

At the Indigenous village of Pavilion, home of the Ts'kw'aylaxw First Nation, the highway veers east and continues through scenic Marble Canyon to reach the modern Cariboo Road, Highway 97, just north of Cache Creek. But, in search of adventure, our road heads straight uphill. In its early days, Pavilion was the site of 22 Mile House, at one time a rip-roaring camp where teamsters and their beasts of burden rested up to prepare for the high climb ahead. Stop at the village for a moment to admire beautiful Holy Trinity Church, built in the 1890s, and then follow the teamsters' route, a two thousand-metre climb over Pavilion Mountain. Today, the steep, unpaved road treks via a series of steep switchbacks through sagebrush and open forest to a high, grassy plateau, great for animal fodder. Stop and look back for the view of misty blue mountain

A market garden on one of the benches, run by the Stswecem'c Xgat'tem First Nation.

ridges, a scene only lightly marred by power-line loops, webs strung across the landscape as if by a gargantuan and energetic spider.

On this huge expanse of surprisingly level tableland, Robert Carson, en route to seek his fortune in the goldfields, noticed the luxuriant bunchgrass, changed his career choice, and took up ranching instead. He homesteaded here, growing hay and raising pigs to sell to the burgeoning settlements along the trail. Today, the ranch is part of the Diamond S cattle ranch; a row of ancient Lombardy poplars and a scattering of buildings mark the old homestead site. Beyond, the road undulates through curvaceous fields, with clumps of aspen in the hollows and wild roses along the fences. The wildflowers up here are lovely. On one of my journeys, fields displayed carpets of blue larkspur and the gold of balsam root sunflowers. It's a bit of a strenuous haul up to these meadows—and down again—but it's worth it.

For years, even after the final Cariboo Road along the Thompson River was finished, miners on foot or on horseback, and even stagecoaches and long trains of freight wagons, travelled this steep, rough road to the goldfields. The River Trail was, after all, a shortcut, though one best travelled in the summer.

Sixteen kilometres from Pavilion, the route across the plateau begins a swift, steep, and serpentine descent, dropping some seven hundred metres in less than six kilometres. So dangerous was this section of narrow road, known as the Rattlesnake Grade, that freight wagons dragged heavy logs to slow them down. If you stop along here, peer out over the cliff edge to catch a glimpse of tiny Pear Lake, twinkling far below. Now preserved within Edge Hills Provincial Park, this little lake in a scoop of flowery meadow provides a small campsite, great fishing, and a sense of lonely quiet—unless the CN freight train whistles through along the nearby tracks. At the bottom of this steep hill, turn left for Pear Lake or right to continue along the gold rush trail.

A short distance along, Kelly Lake fills the valley floor, leaving room only for the road on one side and the railway on the other. Downing Provincial Park at its northern end is a good place to take a break. The lake was named for pioneer rancher Edward Kelly, who settled here in 1886 where the old ranch still stands. Here, the gold rush trail (signposted to Jesmond and Big Bar Ferry) turns northwest up Porcupine Creek into the forested valley that runs between the Edge Hills and the white limestone peaks of the Marble Range. Devoid of trees, these mountain ridges appear snow-covered all year long.

Ducking in and out of power-line clearings, and past a couple of guest ranches, the trail continues to Jesmond, where the old lodging house, made of logs and with a comfortable front porch, sits in a shady hollow. This plot was originally settled in 1870 by Phil Grinder, who called his establishment Mountain House. In 1919, when Henry Coldwell opened a post office here, he was asked to provide a more distinctive postal address and chose Jesmond, the name of his English birthplace. In drowsy summer, with wild roses spilling

FOLLOWING SPREAD Many of the benches are used for hayfields. Some are left to run wild with colourful wildflowers.

ABOVE This enormous log barn at Alkali Lake is one of the oldest along the gold rush trail.

OPPOSITE Alkali Lake Ranch barn doors.

over the fences that line the winding road, Jesmond still exudes an old world charm. At Coldwell Ranch today, there is no post office (it closed in 1965) and no store (it closed in 1970), just a row of mailboxes and some fine old ranch buildings.

North of Jesmond, a signposted road leads west for nineteen kilometres to the Big Bar ferry across the Fraser, one of the few cable reaction ferries still operating in southern BC. It dates back to 1893, operates from April to November (it closes for winter ice), and is on call from 7 a.m. to 7 p.m., with a modest break for lunch. The road down to the ferry is worth a detour: along it there's a schoolhouse, amazing blue and yellow cliffs, volcanic pinnacles, and a few deserted ranch buildings. Near the ferry, irrigated fields are a brilliant green. More adventurous travellers might like to cross the river here and explore the several rough routes that lead, somewhat circuitously, back to Lillooet via the West Pavilion and Yalakom roads.

The Gold Rush River Trail journeys on along the east side of the Fraser, crosses Big Bar Creek, and continues north. Nearby, Big Bar

Moving cattle near Dog Creek.

Guest Ranch has renovated log accommodations dating from the 1940s, but older, and of more historical interest, are the OK Ranch buildings that huddle among a maze of fences in a sweetly curving dip of the old road. This was one of BC's first ranches. Founded by Joseph Haller in 1859, it did double duty as a roadhouse called simply Haller's. Known as the OK Ranch since 1933, its old log buildings and their position right beside the road make this one of the most appealing places along the route.

The ranch is active in a provincial program to restore the habitat of the Columbia sharp-tailed grouse, once the most abundant grouse in North America and now the most threatened, because of shrinking grasslands. This species is known for its courtship displays, performed in spring on traditional dancing grounds known as leks.

A few kilometres beyond the ranch, two major back roads connect east to Highway 97, the first leading to Big Bar Lake and the second to White and Meadow Lakes. Stay left at both intersections. The River Trail then squeezes through a tight limestone canyon, its walls pitted with small caves, and comes out into a wide expanse of irrigated meadow sloping down to the Fraser River and the village of

Beehives at Alkali Lake.

Canoe Creek (Sexqeltqin). Still well above the river, past the ranch house and barns of the BC Cattle Company, the road cuts through a steep, knife-edged, grassy ridge (a glacial esker) and rises up to what seems like the top of the world. Spread out below, the view of the sprawling Fraser River, coiling far below through a turbulent landscape of wrinkled hills and immense sweeps of sagebrush, is unforgettable. The distance seems endless, the scale magnificent—a car on the snail-trail of the road below is a tiny speck, a puff of dust. This dramatic landscape is quietly arrayed in sombre shades of ochre, grey, and soft green, with fiery rocks across the river and sudden jolts of seasonal colours—the flaunt of a fall aspen, a strip of vivid green beside an irrigation ditch, a tuft of rabbit brush. The Fraser River, at the bottom of its deep trench, is supercharged. Can you hear it roar?

The closest the winding gold rush trail comes down to the river level is several kilometres farther along, on the bluffs opposite Churn Creek, where a long, narrow bridge connects the Cariboo to the Chilcotin Country. The road across is signposted to the historic Gang Ranch. Drive down the steep, zigzag road, cross the bridge and look down on the river. You absolutely must do this. The river is mesmerizing.

Back across the Fraser, the gold rush trail climbs steeply and circuitously, coiling around steep gullies on the wide, dry, sagebrush benches. But on one of these benches, notable because it still houses a sod-roofed log cabin, a former hayfield has been turned into the very productive community and market garden of the Canoe Creek-Dog Creek First Nation (Stswecem'c Xgat'tem, or SXFN for short). An amazing burst of colour and fresh greenery in this semi-desert area, the garden is the source of Petak Produce (petak means "potato"), which grows vegetables for Elders and sells its produce at local farmers' markets in the area. Irrigation water comes from nearby Spring Gulch.

From here the road climbs up onto the dry, forested plateau, and then slides down again into the Dog Creek Valley, a serene tapestry of irrigated fields backed by the sheer basalt hulk of Dog Creek Dome. The community of Dog Creek claims a venerable history. A roadhouse was built here in 1856 by Mexican immigrant Raphael Valenzuela; Frenchman Pierre Colin took out a water licence for irrigation in 1861; and later, the Comte de Versepeuch, a French aristocrat, built a waterwheel to generate power for a sawmill. The comte built a large, fancy house and reputedly traded his elegant court clothes—his tricorne hat and blue satin jacket—to Chief Alexis for a string of horses. Later still, a gristmill was installed, the first in the Interior. In 1868, J.S. Place took over the roadhouse, advertised "the finest wines, liquor and cigars," provided stabling for twenty-five horses, and started the Dog Creek Stage Lines, the first in BC to be officially licensed.

Dog Creek kept going when other settlements on the old River Trail faded. Right up until the 1970s there was a post office and well-stocked general store beside the road and the Dog Creek Stage still made twice-weekly trips to Williams Lake in an old blue bus. It was a welcome break along the dusty road. Like so many other gold-rush relics, the store burned down. All that is left here is a huge barn and few apple trees.

Turn right here to visit the Indigenous village of Dog Creek (Xgat'tem), a thriving small community with a school, gas station, general store, and beautiful old church painted a deep and vibrant

An old log cabin near Springhouse.

blue. The community was here long before the gold rush began. The First People had villages and fishing sites all along the river, and at the back of a cavern hidden at the foot of the sheer basalt escarpment that marks the edge of the Dog Creek Dome there are ancient pictographs. Painted in red ochre, the figures of men, a dog, and perhaps a ruffed grouse provide enigmatic links to a past so distant, the gold rush seems as yesterday. The cave and paintings are sacred and can be visited only with a guide. Enquire at the Band Office in the village.

Return to the River Trail and continue north. The road meanders through irrigated meadows below the cliffs then climbs onto high, dry benches above the river. In summer, hiding among the sagebrush are pale purple mariposa lilies, like three-petalled tulips. Keep a lookout for traces of history: old fences, barns, corrals. One fall, camels were billeted here in a log corral—a link to history indeed. They had been brought into this semi-desert area for a movie. Did the movie producers realize that camels were used as pack animals along this very road during the gold-rush era? Did they hear the echoes of history?

At about thirty kilometres from Dog Creek, the road leaves the river benches and angles east into the valley of Alkali Creek, where irrigated fields of grain and alfalfa provide a vibrant contrast to hills the soft colour of buckskin. Alkali Lake, a large dimple in this bowl of green, has been set aside as the Reidemann Wildlife Sanctuary. Here you can see many different species of ducks and geese, and even white pelicans flying through on their way to nesting grounds in the Chilcotin. The lake itself is not alkaline: it was named because of a significant white rock outcrop in the hills nearby.

Alkali Lake Ranch buildings are strung along both sides of the road near the head of the valley. Established in 1861 on the site of an earlier gold-rush roadhouse, it claims to be the oldest ranch in the province. The main house is set back from the road, but jostling your elbows as you drive through are sturdy old log barns (a beam in the biggest one is inscribed with the date 1891), a log cabin that housed the store and post office, and other small buildings. On a bluff overlooking the valley, the Indigenous village of Esk'et celebrates its roots with an annual powwow and a rodeo, two expressions of its heritage. Along its main street is a fine old church, St. Theresa of the Child Jesus, built in 1890 to replace the earlier log structure of 1862, a building that many of the gold seekers must have seen.

Just beyond Esk'et, watch for a narrow track marked Stagecoach Road. This is a stretch of the original trail. It loops around, past a B&B called Esk'et Tiny House, and climbs back onto the main road and out to the Cariboo Plateau, a relatively flat area of meadowland and forest. Twenty-four kilometres from Alkali Lake, the dusty dirt road yields finally to blacktop. At the end of a long day, it might be tempting to drive the rest of the way to Williams Lake without stopping, but the countryside is lovely and it is well worth taking some time to enjoy it. Along with several small lakes loud with ducks in nesting season, there are log fences, meadows, and old buildings to catch the eye. At Springhouse, there is an airstrip for small bush planes, and a pioneer school, now a community hall. The earliest gold rush trails led east through the Chimney Creek valley. But this version of the River Trail continues on pavement for ten kilometres and enters Williams Lake via Highway 20. This town, with its cowboy ambience, is a good place to end the day.

Churn Creek Bridge across the Fraser River.

SIDE TRIP:
ACROSS THE FRASER TO THE GANG RANCH

If you have more time for this adventure, a short side trip across the Churn Creek Bridge near Dog Creek leads to an ancient petroglyph rock and to the historic Gang Ranch.

At the top of the hill across the bridge, the road divides: the left-hand road, signposted for Empire Valley, leads into the Churn Creek protected area, a large expanse of multi-elevation grasslands. While access is limited to a few roads, you can drive along the scenic east side benches above the river, cross the creek, and continue to a picnic area where Stswecem'c Xgat'tem people have set up a small interpretive booth near a large, very sacred boulder inscribed with petroglyphs of men and various inscrutable designs.

Found by a prospector in 1926, the boulder was dragged by a team of ten horses up to the railway near Clinton for transport to Vancouver, where it was put on display in Stanley Park and later moved to the Vancouver Museum. In 1992, this cultural icon was repatriated, shipped back on a large flatbed truck, and replaced on the very same site it came from, its position located by studying old photographs. A signage

Gang Ranch headquarters.

board explains everything. This is a great spot for a picnic: there are tables and a washroom here.

A right turn at the junction across the Churn Creek Bridge will take you up to a wide, flat bench covered with hayfields and on to the historic Gang Ranch with its barns, machinery, and graceful old house. All the roofs are red, giving the place a cheerful aspect. One of BC's oldest and largest ranches, it was so named, it is thought, because it was the first in the west to use a multiple furrow, or gang plough, shipped in from England. It was founded in 1865 by two brothers, Jerome and Thaddeus Harper, who originally mined for gold at Horsefly (Harper's Camp). The Gang's cattle brand, an interlinked JH, dates from this era.

The road through the ranch is accessible to the public, but drive slowly, stay out of the way of farm machinery, and watch for cattle on the move. Once past the ranch, turn left along Reservoir Road, which meanders up the hill to a series of lakes dammed to provide irrigation

A sacred petroglyph, repatriated from the Vancouver Museum, is now restored close to its original site.

water. From this high point, the view of tiny red ranch roofs and blue lakes, all swamped in an immense landscape of enfolding hills, is one to remember.

A network of logging roads leads through the ranchlands to meet up with another bridge, this time across the Chilcotin River, in famously scenic Farwell Canyon. (See page 190.)

4. | **SODA CREEK**
  | A HISTORY REMEMBERED

Soda Creek is one of several small towns that the Cariboo Gold Rush created—and then abandoned. It mushroomed beside the Fraser River at the start of easy river transport north, and was for a brief moment the end of the first Cariboo Wagon Road. Early gold-rush traffic had to stop here and transfer, after a boisterous wait, to paddlewheel steamers bound for Quesnel and the last rough road to the mines. The narrow bench beside the Fraser was quickly crammed with hotels and boarding houses, mills for flour and lumber, general stores, a school, and all the paraphernalia of an important supply centre—even a jail. The steamers made regular trips and the town boomed, its business waning only a little when the wagon road was pushed through all the way to Barkerville. By then the river port of Soda Creek had become a vital link in the development of northern British Columbia, and it remained so for sixty years.

Today, it is barely on the map. Well away from Highway 97 and accessible only by unpaved tracks, it has no store, no gas station, and only a few houses along the single riverside street. There

OPPOSITE This old sod house on the outskirts of Soda Creek has a fine river view. The photo was taken several years ago; hardly anything remains of the house today.

Rudy Johnson's bridge, bought second-hand from Alaska in 1968.

seems little reason besides curiosity to make the journey there. But if you have a feeling for history, this is one little place you must visit.

Start in downtown Williams Lake at the old railway station (now an art gallery and teashop) at the end of Oliver Street. Turn north here along Mackenzie Avenue, which parallels the Fraser through a semi-industrial area and then turns onto Soda Creek Road. The city street soon becomes a quiet shady track that twists with the river and runs along high terraces made when the river was young and less entrenched. Some of these silty terraces have been eroded into hoodoos.

Appropriately for a road named Soda Creek, after nineteen kilometres it crosses Whiskey Creek, and a short distance farther, Stack Valley Road makes a couple of switchbacks down to a bridge across the Fraser—a bridge with a history. Rudy Johnson's Buckskin Ranch lay just across the river and bringing his cattle to market at Williams Lake entailed trucking them sixty kilometres by way of Meldrum Creek or making numerous trips across a former ferry near Soda

Creek. Rudy knew a bridge would be a great solution, and when his wife, Helen, nearly drowned one day when she fell off the ferry, his mind was made up. He bought a second-hand bridge from Alaska. It was dismantled into three thousand pieces, shipped here, reconstructed beside the river, and maneuvered into position, all at his own cost, a total of $200,000—in 1968. Rudy figured he might break even on the deal by levying a toll fee for logging trucks and other commercial vehicles, and so the bridge became the only privately owned toll bridge in BC.

The financial outcome of his venture is not known, but the BC government later bought the bridge and it is now part of the highway system. Drive down to the river here to applaud this example of local enterprise. The bridge provides access to the unpaved Westside Road, which runs north all the way to Quesnel, and south to Highway 20, the Chilcotin road to Bella Coola.

Soda Creek Road stays on the east side of the river, sharing space with the Canadian National Railway, and sometimes ducking underneath it. The railway is a relative newcomer, built here in 1914 as the Pacific Great Eastern Railway and now part of the Great Northern Railway. Past Springfield Ranch, with its big meadows, barns, and homestead, the road runs alternately through grassland and forest, sometimes very close and always very high above the river on cliffs of glacial sediment. A bridge over Hawks Creek marks the spot where the first Cariboo Wagon Road came down to the river from 150 Mile House.

About thirty kilometres from Williams Lake, the road divides: right goes east back to Highway 97, and straight ahead an arrow points the way to the heritage village of Xatśūll on a grassy bench just above the river's canyon. It is an ancient village site, recreated by today's Secwépemc people. The tipis here are not culturally appropriate to the area, but they provide interesting accommodation for visitors. On the site are more historically accurate structures: two kekulis (semi-underground winter houses), a summer house of

FOLLOWING SPREAD A reconstruction of a Secwépemc fishing village right above the river near Soda Creek, with tipis for overnight camping.

ABOVE A cairn was built at Soda Creek in 1958 to celebrate its one hundredth year, and also the BC Centennial.

OPPOSITE The only original building left today along the main street is the log jail.

willow saplings (covered when needed with evergreen boughs), salmon-drying racks, a sweat lodge, and fire-pits. The people of the river lived and thrived in such places long before Europeans set foot in the area.

Archaeologists have determined that the river bench has been a gathering place for at least two thousand years, and Indigenous people still come here to net salmon and participate in sweat lodge ceremonies. Young people gather to learn the old ways, the Elders to remember them. A short distance down the slope, under an enormous fir, is a rock inscribed with ancient petroglyphs.

The heritage village is open to visitors from May to October for guided tours of varying lengths, and for cultural immersion sessions. You can also come here simply to camp. The sound of the river will lull you to sleep. It's an interesting location for a family weekend. For information, see xwistentours.ca.

The jail still has its small barred window.

From Xatśūll, return to the junction and head up the hill to the highway, a diversion made necessary when a great landslide destroyed the bridge over Soda Creek, taking such a huge bite out of the landscape that the road along the river here may never be replaced. The modern Indigenous village nearby is also partly abandoned because of this disaster. At the highway, drive north for three kilometres, then turn left (west) and then left again at the first intersection onto the Soda Creek Townsite Road, which loops back toward the river near a large rock cairn built to honour Soda Creek's historic past and to celebrate BC's centennial in 1959. Near here is the town cemetery, where the most prominent marker is a marble obelisk carved with typically Victorian drapery at the grave of Captain Frank Odin, who died of a heart attack at the wheel of his ship, the SS *Charlotte*, in 1899.

The road swings right, down the main street of the town—or what is left of it. The first Cariboo Wagon Road of 1863 ended here, and supplies and passengers embarked on the SS *Enterprise*, the first of several steamships. Its engine and boilers were transported from the coast by mule train from Port Douglas, and the ship was built on the river near here by G.B. Wright, the road contractor, at a cost of

Down on the river flats, a small market garden, Puddle Produce, grows fresh vegetables for local farmers' markets.

$75,000. It was money well spent: in less than two years Wright had tripled his investment.

Soda Creek had two taverns, two gristmills, a sawmill, and a commodious hotel, a two-storey affair built of logs by Peter Dunlevy, who also owned the store and had a ranch along the river. By 1882, the town had grown, adding a second hotel, a telegraph service, and a post office. Eleven years later, it had stagecoach service to Barkerville and Ashcroft and twice-weekly boats to Quesnel and higher upriver to service the gold mines farther north. By 1945, there were 175 residents, who boasted of the town's Everglades Country Club. But only six years later, a tourist account of the village described it derisively: there were only a couple of primitive stores and a gas station.

Today, even these are gone. There is no longer a wharf or a smart hotel or a gristmill. Only a few houses remain. The country club that used to stand at the end of the road survived for quite some time before it collapsed under a heavy snowfall. Only the town jail, built of sturdy logs in the early 1900s, its small barred windows still intact, remains to tell a story. Its builder, Billy Lynn, became

OPPOSITE A prominent grave in the local cemetery is for Captain Frank Odin of the ss *Charlotte*, who died in 1899.

ABOVE The nearby Indigenous village at Soda Creek was forced to move when the edge of its high terrace was undercut by floods. This sturdy log house remains, but likely not for long.

its first prisoner. Apparently, when his job was finished, Billy went to his favourite saloon to celebrate, imbibed too freely, and was carted off by Constable Robert Pyper to spend the night behind bars that he himself had installed.

Soda Creek, an important piece of the mosaic that is the Cariboo gold-rush story, is not yet a complete ghost town. With its attractive location beside the Fraser River, perhaps it never will be. Growing conditions are great down here by the river. In this favoured microclimate, the local gardens are awash with giant sunflowers, and the town is currently the home of a local enterprise named Puddle Produce, which grows bumper crops of fresh vegetables for farmers' markets in Williams Lake and the surrounding area. You can see the garden below the street, on the river flats.

Return up the road toward the highway, but first, turn left along Soda Creek-Macalister Road, which used to lead back a fair distance north along the river to Highway 97 until it, too, was washed out. It is well worth a quick side trip at least as far as the old Dunlevy Ranch. Still in the cattle ranching business, it is also the home of Soda Creek Sweet Corn. Fifteen acres of ranch fields are now run as a U-pick enterprise for corn and other fresh vegetables that attract customers from miles around.

SIDE TRIP
THE ONWARD RANCH

The cowboy city of Williams Lake, famous for its rip-roaring stampede sits in the middle of great ranchland scenery—and much goldrush history. Up and down Highway 97 there are heritage sites from the 108 Ranch and 150 Mile House to the south and to pioneer roadhouses and ranches all the way north to Quesnel. It makes a great centre for touring

Near to town, at the east end of Williams Lake (the lake) the lively Indigenous village of Sugar Cane is one place to visit and just a few kilometres farther along a scenic backroad through the San Jose River valley is the Onward Ranch, still in business since gold rush days.

The village of Sugar Cane lies away from the highway at the top of the hill just an few kilometres south of Williams Lake. The first settlement here was in 1884, a site chosen by people of the Secwépemc Nation because the sweet grass of the surrounding meadowland was just perfect for their horses.

The village was built around the beautiful Church of the Immaculate Conception, known for its outstanding architecture and detailed craftsmanship. Its facade has been described as "the epitome of balanced design," with two Gothic windows flanking a recessed central doorway beneath a bullseye window. It is known as the last example of Cariboo-style Indigenous church architecture. Built in 1895 by the Oblate Fathers, it is one of the prettiest in the Cariboo. It has been well cared for, was renovated in 2013, and is still the centre of the village where several very old log buildings are being restored.The road runs alongside the large, well-tended graveyard with its central arbor. If you look around, you will spot a few well-carved memorials, two in the form of clan emblems, an eagle and a bear.

It's only a few kilometres south along the unpaved rural backroad to the Onward Ranch, with its big Victorian-style house and huge red barn. Established in 1867 by Charles Eagle and his wife Anna Tatkwa its name came from the declaration by Charles: "This ranch will always go onward!" And it has. Almost 150 years old, it is still going strong. It is now under the ownership of Ty and Ingrid Johnston who manage a large grass-fed herd and sell some of their meat right on site, along with local produce, in the old general store. They keep bees for honey and hold concerts and dances in the landmark barn. And with four children around the place there is lots of action. Visitors are welcome but should keep out of the way of ranch activities.

Like others in the Cariboo, the Onward has stories to tell. Situated beside the first miners' trail, which cut over the hills from the Fraser en route to the gold camps via 150 Mile House (see page 133), the Eagles and their ten children lived at first in a small log house. In the early 1880s they built a small general store, using lumber from their own steam-driven sawmill, and in 1886, they constructed the large Onward House, which became a stopping house along the road to the gold fields. When Charlie Eagle died, the ranch was sold to John Moore and his wife Annie Chiaro. In 1911, the couple built the huge Onward barn, a magnificent structure that soon became a local landmark.

Next to own the ranch were Charles and Vivien Cowan, and during the 1940s the iconic red barn was immortalized on canvas many times by such artists as A.Y. Jackson, Joe Plaskett, and others of Canada's famous Group of Seven, invited to the ranch by Vivien, who had met them at the Banff School of Fine Arts.

Later in this family saga, Sonia, the Cowans' eldest daughter, married Hugh Cornwall, whose family founded Ashcroft Manor, and they took over the management of the ranch. Sonia's artistic talents, encouraged by A.Y. Jackson, soon surfaced, and despite having ranch work to do and children to look after, she managed to keep painting. Her work, well-muscled renditions of ranch life and Cariboo scenery, became well known. By the time she died in 2006, her paintings were in demand worldwide.

The ranch meadows here could very easily inspire an artist: edged with wildflowers and loud with squabbling red-winged blackbirds, they can have changed little since Jackson and Cornwall painted them. The road through the ranch, the original miners' trail, goes beside the barn and the store, crosses the San Jose River, and runs through fields to the railway (once the Pacific Great Eastern, then BC Railway, now the Canadian National) and the site of the old Onward Station.

The family live in the Onward ranch house, a very pretty 19th century yellow and white cottage. The oldest building on the ranch, the general store, now renovated, dates right back to gold rush days.

5. | LILLOOET TO PEMBERTON
LAKES AND RIVERS

The scenery around Lillooet has a decidedly vertical thrust. Surrounded by mountains deeply incised by tributary rivers that hurtle down to meet the Fraser in its own steep and twisting canyon, this is a visually stunning landscape, and a particularly interesting one because the geology is divided: west of the Fraser lie the peaks of the Coast Mountains, and to the east, the older mountains at the edge of the Fraser Plateau.

An adventurous circle drive from Lillooet follows the Bridge River to the reservoir of Carpenter Lake, crosses the top of the Mission Dam, and climbs over a high divide to Seton and Anderson Lakes. Then up and down again over the well-named Highline Road to join Highway 99 at Pemberton for the return journey. This route is scenic, wild, and historic—a perfect combination.

Lillooet is strung out on a series of high glacial terraces above the Fraser River beside its confluence with Cayoosh Creek. It is one of the oldest towns in British Columbia, dating from the gold-rush days of the 1860s, but 150 years of European history is nothing compared to the Indigenous presence here. At Keatley Creek, just twenty kilometres north, archaeologists from Simon Fraser University

OPPOSITE The confluence of the Bridge and Fraser Rivers is a traditional fishing area for the St'át'imc people. They know it as Xwísten.

uncovered a fishing village of 115 pit houses that had been lived in continuously for fifteen hundred years. Beneath the village, remains were found of even older settlements dating back seven thousand years.

The confluence of the Bridge and the Fraser Rivers has always been a culturally important place to the St'át'imc Nation. They knew it as Xwísten, or "smiling place," and lived comfortably on the riches of the river, catching salmon in the rapids and curing them on racks hung in the hot winds that still blow along the canyons. This air-dried salmon, called tswan, provided food for the winter and was produced in such quantities that surplus was available for trade.

The first Europeans to infiltrate this self-sufficient society came with Simon Fraser, who staggered through in 1808 asking for help to bring their canoes through the Fraser rapids and for advice on how to reach the Pacific. According to Fraser's reports, he was met near Cayoosh Creek by an assembly of one thousand, treated kindly, given provisions, and sent on his way. Fraser and his voyageurs were the first Europeans the original inhabitants had seen, and the historic encounter lives on in old stories.

After Fraser's visit, apart from the yearly passage of the fur brigades, little changed in the lives of the St'át'imc people until the Fraser River and Cariboo gold rushes, some fifty years later. The two first miners' trails up from the coast converged here on the Fraser, where the Indigenous village was overrun by Europeans. The shanty town they built here, Cayoosh or Lillooet, became Mile "0," the start of the road to Cariboo's gold.

There is so much history in and around Lillooet that you could very well stay a while before heading out on this circular journey. At the very least, take a walking tour of the town and spend some time beside the old suspension bridge that crosses the Fraser at the foot of Main Street. This bridge, now a provincial heritage site, was built in 1913, replacing a simple truss bridge that had in turn superseded

OPPOSITE Logging trucks use the road, so expect dust in summer. This truck was coming down from the Pavilion Forest Road, just by the Bridge River crossing.

a winch ferry built in 1860. Restored for foot traffic only, the bridge provides a good view of the river—and a great home for the local bats. Eight species of bats, five of them on the endangered list, are known to live in the area, and the Lillooet Naturalist Society has installed several bat boxes under the bridge deck as roosting places. Come at dusk to watch the bats fly.

The bridge was built over the river at a traditional fishing hole for the Fraser's rare white sturgeon, a gigantic fish that has amazingly lived on, virtually unchanged, since Jurassic times. The sturgeon here, now under catch-and-release protection, make up the only known wild stock of the species in Canada, one of only three populations in the world. (The others are on the Sacramento and the Columbia Rivers in the United States.)

Our journey heads north from Lillooet along the west bank of the Fraser, past a few old farms and orchards on the river terrace. The river is far below, twisting through a deep canyon full of rapids. At about six kilometres from town, the Bridge River cuts through a narrow rock canyon of its own, its glacial waters a clear, deep blue-green, an astonishing contrast to the muddy brown Fraser into which it flows. There is space for parking on the river side of the road at the confluence just before the Bridge River bridge, but be considerate: this is Xwísten territory and their prime fishing spots are nearby. If you venture out along some of the short trails leading to the river's edge, you might see, if the season is right, racks of salmon drying in the wind under tarps, or people fishing. The thirty-metre-wide canyon just above where the rivers join is Sxetl, or "the drop-off," and you will see that it was aptly named.

Archival photos show people fishing here with dip nets and spears, hunkered down on frail-looking planks suspended high over the river, or standing precariously on water-splashed rocks. There is still a strong fishery here, and from June to September the

OPPOSITE Lillooet is surrounded by steep, rocky mountains. This is the view from the historic town graveyard.

FOLLOWING SPREAD Hydraulic mining created this huge chasm beside the river.

This road follows the Bridge River to the Mission Dam.

Xwísten community provides tours of the site and, just upriver, of an ancient village site of eighty pithouses, one of them reconstructed. For information, phone 250-256-0673 or see xwistentours.ca. The community is also involved in the Apple Springs salmon habitat restoration project, higher up the Bridge River.

Cross the Bridge River, which took its name from a toll footbridge for gold-rush travellers, and head through the dry pine forests. Just past the intersection with Joseph Road are the remains of the ancient pithouse village, a huge array of circular depressions, like giant dimples, on a sagebrush bench above the river. You must not trespass on the meadow here, but you can stop and look over the site. Conditions on the road along the valley vary: some parts are wide and easy, others narrow, twisting, and very close to the canyon's edge. It is a mainline forestry road, so watch out for logging trucks.

One amazing sight is a gigantic semicircular chasm on a river bend, the remains of a hydraulic mining operation that cut though

ABOVE This road to Seton Portage climbs up to a narrow bridge across the top of the Mission Dam, then enters a short tunnel.

FOLLOWING SPREAD Carpenter Lake backs up behind the dam. The road on the left goes to Bralorne; on the right, to Seton Portage.

towering cliffs of sand and clay. Luckily there is room on the shoulder to pull over and enjoy the spectacle. A nearby trail leads precariously down to the river.

About thirty kilometres from Lillooet, Yalakom Road turns east to the old settlement of Moha, now long gone but still listed as one of BC's ghost towns. Just past this intersection, a series of plunging hairpin bends brings the road down to cross the Yalakom River and follow Bridge River up into its narrow canyon. After full sun exposure on the high road, the forested cool of the canyon beside the river, overhung with waterfalls and steep talus slopes, is a pleasant change.

The riverside Mission Dam Recreation Area at the head of the canyon is a good place for a picnic, under the spillway of the huge

Anderson Lake looking south from Seton Portage.

Terzaghi Dam. (Mission is its colloquial name.) The dam backs up the Bridge River to form a long reservoir known as Carpenter Lake, which stretches for fifty-five kilometres northwest and is bordered by another adventure road (for next time) which goes all the way to Gold Bridge and Bralorne, old towns dating from a later gold rush.

Our route turns left at an intersection signposted for Seton Portage. The road is single lane as it leads right across the top of the dam and through a short tunnel to emerge on the far side of Carpenter Lake.

The topography of this dramatic mountain area proved perfect for hydroelectric projects. The upper Bridge River Valley is nearly 550 metres above Seton Lake, which lies almost directly below it on the other side of Mission Mountain. This huge difference in elevation was put to good use when engineers built the dam and sent the impounded water into a diversion tunnel through the mountain and down to powerhouses on Seton Lake. Other hydroelectric dams on

A warning sign as the Highline Road starts its climb up and along Anderson Lake.

the upper river, and later on the Seton River, followed soon afterwards. All this dam construction resulted in Bridge River water being used three times for the production of electricity before being discharged back into the Fraser via Seton River.

The environmental costs were enormous. The damage to Bridge River fisheries; the flooding of a productive river valley and its First Nations and pioneer settlements; and the degradation of once-pristine Seton Lake, a freshwater fiord once noted for its clear sky-blue waters are all things to think about as you start the steep climb up Mission Mountain.

The journey from Carpenter Lake to Seton Lake is only twenty kilometres, but give yourself some time. The climb up to the summit is a reasonably easy mountain drive, but coming down is not. An aerial view of the road shows a faint skinny line looping in sharp, precipitous zigzags down through steep forests to the lakeshore. It is hard to believe that this frail link was once the only access route

ABOVE An old sign, from when upkeep was done by locals.

OPPOSITE The steep start down the twisting road.

from the railway below to the gold mines of the Upper Bridge River. Along its 14 percent grades came all the goods, supplies, machinery, and workers needed in the townsites of Bralorne, Pioneer, Gold Bridge, and Minto. When the hydroelectric projects began later, convoys of trucks travelled the same road, hauling heavy machinery up almost twelve hundred metres to the ridge summit and then steeply down to the dam site.

Today's descent down this road is a challenge, and not recommended for those pulling long trailers or with little experience of mountain driving. The grades are steep, the curves very sharp—there are at least eight hairpin bends—and in places the road is not only narrow but also perched on the edge of the steep mountainside. This invigorating road, a shorter rival to Bella Coola's Big Hill (see page 203), is the only one linking Seton Portage to Lillooet. Locals think nothing of driving up and back for groceries or doctor's visits, even in winter.

At the end of the descent, about seventy-five kilometres from Lillooet, the road splits: left leads to Shalalth, right to Seton Portage.

Another government warning sign.

The latter was known until 1959 as Short Portage (to differentiate it from the Cariboo Trail's Long Portage, between Anderson and Lillooet Lakes). These long mountain lakes were once a single freshwater fiord almost fifty kilometres long, curving between the Bendor and Cayoosh ranges of the Coast Mountains. About ten thousand years ago, tectonic movement along a nearby fault line triggered a giant landslide that blocked the valley, dividing the lake into two sections. In 1861, along the five-kilometre isthmus between the lakes, Karl Dozier built BC's first railway, a crude affair that used mules to pull wagons on wooden rails from one wharf to another along the first gold rush trail.

Once down the hill at lake level, the road to Shalalth follows the Canadian National Railway tracks along the shore, but there is no mainline passenger service. Until recently, the Seton Lake Band, in conjunction with the CN, ran a local train (known as the Kaoham Shuttle) between Shalalth and Lillooet with two passenger cars, but the service has, for the moment at least, been discontinued, and Mission Hill Road is presently the only way to go.

From Shalalth, the road to Seton Portage dodges under the huge black pipes that bring water through the mountain and down to the hydroelectric power plant. The concrete supports are decorated with Indigenous motifs painted in red and black. At the start of Seton Portage village, turn left at a sharp bend in the road to reach the site of the old steamship wharf, passing St. Mary's Church, one of BC's oldest, and today so frail it is only the ghost of a church. Condemned as unsafe years ago, it was scheduled to be razed, but the Elders of the community wanted it left to disintegrate in its own time, as coastal totem poles do.

The land between Seton and Anderson Lakes, sheltered by high mountains and warmed by the lakes, enjoys a microclimate surprisingly akin to that of the Mediterranean. Snowfall is meagre and the alluvial soil fertile. Gardens thrive here, and at one time the area was known for its fine orchards, some of which survive. Locals think of it as a Shangri-La, almost cut off from the rest of the world. The community is loosely spread out along the original gold-rush portage trail of 1858, still the only main road through the isthmus. Travellers can find a few facilities here, including a large new hotel, a general store, and the Highline Pub & Restaurant. A restored train caboose houses the tourist centre in the small Seton Lake Provincial Historic Park, where a sign commemorates BC's first crude railway.

The main road crosses the Whitecap River at the south end of the village, sweeping around to a shingle beach at the south end of the portage. Anderson Lake is clear and dark blue, reflecting the receding ridges of the high mountains that surround it. There are no valley edges here: the mountains drop steeply down into what is geologically a freshwater fiord. The railway tracks alongside the

FOLLOWING SPREAD From the Highline Road, a great view of the two lakes, Anderson and Seton.

lake had to be carved into steep cliffs along the shore. No wonder that most of the gold-rush traffic between Pemberton and Seton Portage went by boat, because the foot trail itself had to forge a twenty-eight-kilometre route that climbed up and down five hundred metres along the mountain side, crossing several gushing streams.

This historic section of gold rush trail is still there. After it fell into disuse it became a track used by the power company to plant its transmission lines down to the coast, and it became unofficially known as the Highline Road. It offered a narrow, unpaved, and difficult trek for backroaders, one of the worst (or best, depending on your preferences). Four-wheel drives were usually required.

Officially Anderson Lake Road, it was looked after for years by Seton Lake residents: it was their only direct route to the coast. Today, it is maintained by BC Highways, which undertook some major reconstruction work in 2020. Riding high above the lake, it is one of the most scenic adventure roads in the province—but check conditions before you start. It is generally closed for winter snows, and there are frequent washouts.

The always scenic, sometimes scary Anderson Lake Road winds down into the little settlement originally known as Port Anderson, then as D'Arcy, and now as the village of N'Quatqua. Heritage Park, at the south end of the lake, marks the finish of the Long Portage from Lillooet Lake and the beginning of steamer travel along Anderson Lake in gold-rush and pre-railway days. It's a good place to unwind after your drive.

The rest of the journey is easy—forty kilometres of paved road all the way to Mount Currie and Pemberton through coastal greenery, lush with salal and cedar, quite a change from the arid pine forests of Lillooet. At Mount Currie, you can head south to Vancouver by way of Whistler and Squamish. But to complete the circle, turn left at the village and head north back to Lillooet along the paved Duffey Lake Road, Highway 99. Be aware that any highway through the BC mountains is prone to extreme weather catastrophes: in the fall of 2021 this road was closed on several occasions because of washouts and landslides. Check conditions in Mount Currie.

A huge pipe carries water from tunnels down to the hydroelectric plant. Indigenous designs brighten its supports.

Just before this highway reaches Lillooet, there's a picnic site and viewpoint high above the western end of Seton Lake. A trail down to the shore here leads to small Seton Lake Campsite, run by BC Hydro, where old acacia trees, planted as memorials to Lillooet's lost men of the First World War, provide welcome shade.

At Lillooet, where the Bridge of the 23 Camels takes Highway 99 across the Fraser en route to Cache Creek and the Cariboo, the circle trip is over. What will you remember most? The daring zigzags of Mission Mountain or the hypnotic greens and blues of the lakes and mountains along the Highline Road?

An Indigenous graveyard along the road to Skatin.

SIDE TRIP:
PILGRIMAGE TO SKATIN

If you have time to spare for a pilgrimage, another adventure road from Mount Currie will take you to a World Heritage Site, one of the most beautiful rural churches in BC at the Indigenous village of Skatin, also known as Skookumchuck. Remote and little visited, it deserves your time and attention.

This side trip begins south of Mount Currie, where the Duffey Lake Road (Highway 99) bridges Lillooet Lake, makes a sharp turn, and zig-zags uphill for the return route to Lillooet. Keep going straight onto an unpaved road, which leads south for sixty kilometres along the shore of Lillooet Lake and River, an original section of the first gold rush trail, known as the Douglas Road, that came up from the Fraser River via Harrison Lake and Port Douglas. It is designated a BC Heritage Road. The past can be experienced here through the bumps and potholes on the trail.

This historic route has been worked over, of course, in the years since the gold rush—it's now the In-SHUCK-ch Forest Service Road, with kilometre markers recording the distance from Mount Currie—but the scenery has not changed. The lake and river route is long and lovely, the forested shoreline very steep, and there is little development along the way beyond four small forest service recreation sites, a lodge, and a B&B. Much of the route leads through reserve lands of the St'át'imc Nation. Near forest road marker 38 there is a small fenced Indigenous graveyard; you'll see another, this one with an ornate Gothic-inspired gateway, at the village of Sweeten, a few kilometres farther south.

If it's a hot summer weekend, you might wonder at the number of family cars and pickups driving along this usually lonely road. They are likely all headed for the hot springs, about forty-six kilometres from Mount Currie, a natural upwelling of scalding water right beside the cold river. With large cedar soaking tubs and a small riverside campsite, the springs are commonly known as Skookumchuck, but their Indigenous name is Tsek. This was, of course, the most popular stop along the miners' trail. Judge Begbie, who made the trip *on foot* from Lillooet to Port Douglas in 1859, named the spring St. Agnes Well, after one of Governor James Douglas's daughters.

Keep on the road that climbs above the hot springs and continue south for another four kilometres to the village of Skatin, at the 19 Mile Post. The huge white Church of the Holy Cross towers over the dusty village street, a miracle of survival: it has been standing here in the damp coastal forest since it was completed in 1905 on the bones of an older church built by Oblate missionaries. There are few other BC churches as old and elegant as this one, and certainly none in such an isolated place. The building is a marvel of Carpenter Gothic architecture, with three tall spires, decorative trim, stained glass windows, everything one could want in a building shown on Google Maps as the "Skookumchuk Cathedral." If you are lucky enough to be allowed inside—check with the Skatin Band Office in Mount Currie—you will be amazed by the beautiful hand-carved woodwork. Look for the white dove, an unusual piece of ecclesiastical folk art, hanging high in the rafters. And take a respectful walk in the graveyard with its inscribed wooden gravestones and decorative metal crosses.

The forestry road continues south all the way to what little remains of the town of Port Douglas at the head of Harrison Lake, but the pilgrimage is over and the road ahead increasingly rough and little travelled. It presently dead-ends at the lake, though there are plans to extend it all the way to Harrison Hot Springs. Stop here, by the church. It is enough to have come so far. What other adventure road ends with a pilgrimage?

OPPOSITE Church of the Holy Cross, World Heritage Site, built in 1905.

6. | FORT ST. JAMES
AN ADVENTURE INTO EARLY HISTORY

Fort St. James, built in 1806, is the oldest of BC's Historic Places, and its site, on the south end of huge Stuart Lake, one of the most beautiful. The community shares space with the Indigenous village of Nak'azdli, an association that began when Simon Fraser established the fur-trading post here, two years before he began his epic journey down the Fraser to the Pacific Ocean.

The Stuart Lake Post, later known as Fort St. James, is now a national historic site and holds the greatest number of original wooden fur-trade buildings in Canada. A visit here would more than justify this scenic detour off Highway 16, near Vanderhoof. But around the bay from the fort is another wonderful landmark, the Church of Our Lady of Good Hope, built by Oblate missionaries in 1873, one of the oldest churches in BC. Farther along the lake are two more Indigenous villages, each with an old church.

The early European development of the northern BC Interior owes much to the fur trade and the explorations of its

OPPOSITE Our Lady of Good Hope, its spire a landmark along the shore.

FOLLOWING SPREAD A view from the fort dock down the huge, lonely expanse of Stuart Lake, once a highway for the voyageurs.

The main trading house of the HBC, its logs still stalwart. Established in 1806, this is the oldest historic place in BC.

employees—adventurers such as Simon Fraser, sent west into uncharted territory to find a navigable river route to the Pacific. Two years after he established the Stuart Lake Post, named for his assistant, John Stuart, he canoed east down the Nechako to its junction with another large river. Mistaking this for the Columbia, he followed it doggedly to the sea. The river was, of course, the Fraser, the same one that Alexander Mackenzie, another fur-trade hero, had started to explore fifteen years earlier before heading west through the Chilcotin to make his heroic overland journey to the Pacific.

The Dakelh or Carrier village of Nak'azdli was located at the intersection of three important Indigenous Peoples' trails at the south end of Stuart Lake where the Necosli River and the much larger Stuart River flow into the lake almost side by side. What better location for a fur-trading post? The Stuart Lake Post (it changed its name when the North West Company merged with the HBC) was the headquarters of the New Caledonia department, and around it grew the village of Fort St. James, the first permanent European

An alternate view of the trading house.

settlement between California and Alaska. The community quickly became a centre for trade and cooperation with the surrounding First Nations and a base for later explorations of the north. In the 1850s, Franklin Pope stayed here while searching out a route for the Collins Overland Telegraph (the prominent white round-topped peak along the lake is named after him) and, later still, miners, loggers, and settlers depended on the fort store for supplies.

The first fur traders depended on the Dakelh not only for the furs that they traded but also for manpower and sustenance. The village chief was Kwah, who had control of extensive beaver lands and maintained a successful fish weir. He kept the new arrivals well supplied with fish, game meat, and other provisions. An acclaimed leader of the Dakelh People, he was known to the Europeans as King of the Carriers. The road leading to the fort is named after him, and his grave is an honoured site beside the lake.

The journey into historic Fort St. James starts where Highway 27 heads north from Highway 16 near Vanderhoof. The first sixty kilometres traverse the comfortable pastoral fields of the Nechako Valley

through the small districts of Prairiedale and Dog Creek. But the pioneer farmland tranquility soon comes to an end. The bridge across the Stuart River at the broad end of the lake marks the switch to a sterner mountainous landscape of water and forests. Stuart Lake is enormous, stretching, beyond the sky it seems, almost one hundred kilometres northwest. It is long and wild, subject to high winds and sudden squalls that make travel by small boat perilous. Surrounded by steep forested slopes, it is part of an unbroken chain of long lakes and rivers extending northwest for more than four hundred kilometres, a huge navigable waterway that formed the basis for the Dakelh way of life. The bridge is a good place to stop in fall to watch salmon migrating upstream, and in winter to watch flocks of trumpeter swans attracted by the open water at the edge of the frozen lake.

The historic fort is beside the lake, right in the centre of the village, and the HBC flag, with the Union Jack in its corner, flaps madly over the old log buildings. Today they are linked by boardwalks through neatly mowed lawns—probably far different from how the fort looked when it was in business. It has a clear view southwest, looking out over wide empty reaches of water, sky, and mountain. How homesick the voyageurs must have been, gazing into this huge, shuddering loneliness.

You will want to spend some time here, for this is where much of BC's European settlement history began. Take the guided tours of the various buildings—five are originals, furnished and supplied as they would have been in the mid-1800s. Site personnel, well versed in fur-trade history and dressed for their eighteenth-century roles, will help to bring the past alive. Outside the large fur storehouse are hand-carved replicas of wooden, Indigenous canoes which were put to good use along the lake chain. The long wharf, now quite frail and no longer in use, dates from 1894 and was regularly used by lake transport steamers until the boats stopped service in 1914.

From the fort, a left turn onto Stuart Drive leads around the lake to Cottonwood Park, where there is a miniature of an old Junkers

OPPOSITE Furs were the backbone of the HBC empire. Their forts were always built in the best trading places.

This miniature of a float plane flies high above lakeside Cottonwood Park, a memorial to the early bush pilots.

float plane set up to commemorate the early days of the bush pilots who helped to open up the country in a much later era. Elsewhere in the village are memorials to Chief Kwah and to Russ Baker, whose bush pilot company grew eventually into Pacific Western Airlines. You can drive from here to see the church (take Lakeshore Road, a turning off the main highway), but a more satisfying approach is to walk from Cottonwood Park around the bay on the stony beach. This will give you time to make the transition from the eighteenth-century world of the fur trade to the later and more difficult missionary period, when the well-meaning introduction of Christianity often did far more harm than good.

The architecture of the white mission Church of Our Lady of Good Hope deserves your attention, mostly because of its tall spire,

Built in 1873, Our Lady of Good Hope is one of the oldest and loveliest in the province.

intricately built with pointed arches, small gables and pinnacles, a landmark seen from far out on the lake. A small church was built here as early as 1869, and four years later a larger one was needed. Traditional oral history tells of the great logs for its construction being hauled five kilometres across the lake ice. The new church was ready by Christmas.

What we see today is a church fairly extensively remodelled in 1905. The tower was extended, the spire added, and those old logs, still in place, covered by siding. In the log cabin behind the church, Father Adrien-Gabriel Morice had a printing press where he produced prayer books and newspapers in a syllabic representation of the Dakelh language, which had no written form until he decided to invent one. He also wrote several books in English, including *The*

OPPOSITE The church tower and spire are strongly Gothic in design. It was remodelled in 1905.

ABOVE Church of the Holy Cross, perhaps the very oldest log church in Canada, sits in the lakeside village of Binche.

History of the Northern Interior of British Columbia, Formerly New Caledonia, 1660–1880, published in 1904 and still a reference classic today. In the large graveyard nearby, the inscriptions on several of the tombstones are written in Dakelh, which looks similar to the glyphs on Egyptian papyrus.

Around the curve of the bay, Lakeshore Drive continues, past the road to the graveyard, to the long dock of Cottonwood Marina. Here you can launch your own canoe and head out on a maritime adventure or arrange a fishing trip or a visit to see First Nations pictographs, painted in red ochre on lakeside cliffs right beside the water's edge.

Farther south along the lake's north shore are two villages of the Tl'azt'en Nation, Pinchi (Binche) and Tachie (Tache). To reach them, drive north a short distance on Highway 26 (also signed as N

Church of St. Kateri above the village of Tachie

Road and Germanson Lake Road) and turn left onto Tachie Road, which climbs up into the forest, cuts right through the huge operations of Apollo Lumber, and then heads southwest, quite high above the lake, behind the bald head of Mount Pope.

The village of Binche lies below the main road, twenty-five kilometres from Fort St. James. It's a neat little settlement whose houses, nearly all of them with lake frontage, are built along several scenic bays. Follow the side road down into the village and turn left, past the Binchie (yes, that's the correct spelling) Bay Store, to road's end, where Pinchi Creek tumbles into the lake. The small park here is a good place for a picnic—there's also a campsite—and right beside the creek is the Church of the Holy Cross, built in 1871 and moved to its present location in 1930. A very small, simple building of squared logs, it is said to be the oldest log church in BC. There's a tiny graveyard in the trees behind.

The village of Tachie, seat of the main office of the Tl'azt'en Nation, lies twenty kilometres farther south. The highway's downhill approach gives a fine view of the village, the lake with its many islands, and the red spire of the fairly modern Church of St. Kateri. St. Cecelia's Church, down the hill, closer to the lake, is much older and still has shingles on its spire and several little ornamental details popular in the Victorian era. Its church bell, very visible in the Gothic arched window in the tower, was shipped over from France and made the long journey from Victoria by ocean, river, lakes, and trails, reaching its final destination by dugout canoe.

This adventure ends here, but if you plan to stay overnight in Fort St. James, one of the best things to do the next day is to hike up Mount Pope, the huge white bluff that you can see along the shore. The trailhead is four kilometres along Stony Bay Road, a left turn from the highway just north of the village. It's a fairly steep trail, seven kilometres and back, with several zigzags, but it's worth the effort: the view from the gazebo on the bald summit is truly spectacular. Rock climbers also come here to pit themselves against the sheer limestone walls. Check in advance: access to the climbing cliffs is sometimes closed when the local peregrine falcons are nesting.

An early stroll along the beach, past the fort and the tall spire of the church, will be an excellent warm-up. Sunrise over the lake is often spectacular.

7. | THE BACK ROAD TO BARKERVILLE

After leaving the path beside the Fraser River, early miners along the first Cariboo gold rush trail pushed north and east to the lakes and rivers beyond Horsefly and Quesnel, encouraged by reports of bedrock covered by deposits of blue clay, a geologic convergence similar to that found in the richest gold strikes of California. They discovered that the land east of the river was very different from the dry open benches on the western side. There were steep mountain valleys thick with jack pine forest, spruce swamps, and a maze of lakes and turbulent rivers. The trails were difficult, and the miners' progress agonizingly slow. And the horseflies (hence the name of the community), and mosquitoes were always hungry.

Gold is not a magnetic mineral, but its lure is strong. Prospecting on every creek on their way, the miners struggled through the thick bush northeast to Quesnel Lake and the Cariboo River, and then upstream to Keithley Creek, one of the earliest of the Cariboo gold camps. From here, the way led over the Snowshoe Plateau and Yanks Peak to the gold rich creeks of Antler and Williams, where, a few years later, the town of Barkerville was born, screaming itself into existence.

OPPOSITE Crosina's store at 153 Mile House, now closed, and a display of old machinery. The road to Barkerville ran right by.

Barkerville was the coveted arrival point for hopeful miners—as it is today for tourists.

This first miners' trail to Barkerville looks far shorter on the map than the official six-metre-wide Cariboo Wagon Road that supplanted it, but the land there was far too difficult for road building. Lieutenant H. Spencer Palmer of the British Royal Engineers, dispatched from New Westminster in 1860 to survey a wagon road to the goldfields, sent back a description of these trails: "Slippery, precipitous ascents and descents, fallen logs, overhanging branches, roots, rocks, swamps, turbid pools and miles of deep mud." This was obviously not his chosen route. Once his Wagon Road was completed—roughly along the route of today's Highways 97 and 24—the old rough trail fell into disuse. Parts of it are still there, waiting to be discovered as an alternative to highway travel if you are looking for a deeper dip into history and quieter roads through the Cariboo hills.

While the original trail over the Snowshoe Plateau to Barkerville is passable only on foot or by four-wheel drive, there is now another option: a forestry road, quite good enough for a two-wheel-drive

The fields and lakes near 150 Mile are a very different landscape from the forested mountains ahead.

vehicle, goes up the east side of Cariboo Lake and over Cameron Ridge to Barkerville via the Matthew River. But be prepared for a rutted or dusty winding road, narrow bridges, and forest all the way from Likely, where the pavement ends.

Start on Highway 97 at 150 Mile House, which began as one of the roadhouses along the Cariboo Road, 150 miles from Lillooet. Though far smaller than it used to be in gold-rush days, it is still a crossroads and still guards a few relics of days past. Beside the highway is the Little Red Schoolhouse, built of wood frame in 1896, still with its furnishings, and open in summer. Also here is the 1913 courthouse, a building barely holding itself together and awaiting heritage restoration. It is surprisingly small, considering that it housed the courtroom, jail, and living accommodation for the town's lone constable. Both buildings are on the Canadian Register of Historic Places.

The Likely Road turns off east just beside the service station. Five kilometres along is one of the most interesting of the old Cariboo places: 153 Mile House. The land here was pre-empted in 1903 by Italian immigrants Louis and Clara Crosina, who at first lived in a small log house where they started a general store. A couple of years later, they built a much larger six-bedroom home, which, because of

FOLLOWING SPREAD All that is left of the once very popular Big Lake Stopping place are the ranch barns. A heritage site, this is a good place for a picnic.

THE BACK ROAD TO BARKERVILLE 133

The riverside village of Likely centres on the hotel and store; it makes a great overnight stop.

Clara's good food and hospitality, became a popular roadhouse. A bed, meals, fodder, and accommodation for horses were all priced at 50 cents apiece. The family enterprise flourished—the roadhouse for thirty-five years, the store for even longer. In 1914, the store was expanded, selling everything from food to dry goods, clothing, hardware, farm machinery, and, later, automobile parts and gasoline.

When the roadhouse closed, the Crosinas' daughter, Lillian, ran the family ranch until she sold the property to the Patenaude family, but she kept the store going until her death in 1963. The store remained as Crosina left it, retaining not only the essence but also the contents of a bygone pioneer era. It could be shown by appointment until the ranch changed hands and the store visits stopped. A section of the original Wagon Road runs through the ranch beside some old log barns, a blacksmith shop, and the store, with a display of old machinery and its original gas pump outside. It's a working ranch, so be respectful if you stop to walk or drive through.

Two kilometres beyond the ranch, the road forks. Keep left on the Likely Road (right leads to Horsefly) and follow the gold-rush

TOP Quesnelle Forks is a ghost town, but one in remission. The old buildings are being restored as a heritage site.

BOTTOM Quesnelle Forks once housed a very large Chinese community. This is the Tong House.

OPPOSITE Seen through a window, Quesnelle Forks has a ghostly air.

ABOVE Keithley Creek, one of the oldest gold camps, has a well-tended graveyard and an adjacent free library.

route to the site of 158 Mile House, once known as Mountain House (there is nothing here now). Here, a later incarnation of the Wagon Road turned and followed Deep Creek (now Hawks Creek) down to the Fraser and the Soda Creek wharf. Here, travellers and freight took passage on a paddle steamer all the way to the mouth of the Quesnel River where the wagon road started again.

The earlier gold rush trail—and the modern highway—veers right and continues for about fifteen kilometres through forest and past aspen-fringed Skulow Lake, then breaks out into meadows rustic with old snake fences, barns, and cabins. The road is paved but quiet, and it is easy to imagine miners and their pack trains clopping along. Past the end of Big Lake the road comes to the small modern community of Big Lake, site of yet another stopping house, this one built in 1896 by William Parker, who ran a stage line and carried the mail from Ashcroft to Quesnelle Forks. The Parker house burned down in 1954, but there are still two old log buildings—a barn and a saddle shed—at this shady heritage site, along with picnic tables and some old farm machinery. Turn down Pritchard Road for access. Big

At the only place along the backroad where one might go wrong, a hand-painted sign marks the way.

Creek has a store and pub and a big volunteer-run fire and rescue building.

Crossing the hump of Limestone Mountain, the Wagon Road made a sharp bend to cross Beaver Creek. The ranch buildings here mark the site of Beaver Lake House, one of the most famous stopping places along the trail. It was established in 1861 by Peter Dunlevy, who made the first gold strike in the Cariboo on the Horsefly River and later amassed a fortune as owner of the hotel at Soda Creek. Miner J.C. Bryant praised Beaver Lake House in his journal of 1863: "The hotel is the best between Victoria and the Cariboo, indeed Victoria hotels could not compare with this one in the splendid meals given to the guests." He continued in rapturous praise of the baked meats, fresh vegetables, huge huckleberry pies, and cream.

Around the hotel were two stores, a gambling hall, and a thriving market for pack animals. All these original buildings have gone, and the site is now occupied by the Hamilton Ranch. Beaver Valley is an attractive place, its meadows knee-deep in dandelions in spring and neatly fenced around the edges. Keep straight on across the bridge for Likely. Beyond, Beaver Valley Road leads southeast to Horsefly, another good backroad.

From here on, the road enters the inland rainforest of the Central Cariboo. Watch for a break in the trees to the right for a glimpse of Moorhead Lake, an artificial reservoir built to provide water storage for the Bullion Mine, once the greatest hydraulic gold mine in the world. In operation from 1897 until 1941, it consumed huge amounts of water. In addition to the reservoir, nearly

ABOVE In the middle of nowhere is a most unusual café.

RIGHT The café terrace below Cameron Ridge looks across to the gold rush mountains near Barkerville.

thirty-five kilometres of ditches were dug to carry water from Bootjack and Polley Lakes. The high-pressure sluicing resulted in a rich sludge that filtered out into millions of dollars' worth of gold, and under the onslaught of powerful hoses the gulch became wider and deeper by the day. Today, what was once called Dancing Bill's Gulch is no longer a gulch but a chasm, three kilometres wide and a hundred metres deep, its gravel sides bright yellow. A rest stop along the road provides an excellent view, and a trail leads to the rim. Some machinery from the site is on view.

The paved road continues to Quesnel Lake, the deepest glacial lake in North America with depths of more than five hundred metres. A relic of the huge linear glaciers that once drained the western flanks of the Cariboo Mountains, it sprawls on the map like an enormous slingshot, its two great arms stretching northeast

OPPOSITE The view from the ridge toward the gold bonanzas in the Cariboo mountains.

into a huge area of mountain wilderness protected by an interlocking string of provincial parks: Wells Gray, Cariboo Mountains, and Bowron Lakes.

Just before the village of Likely, the road bridges the lake's gushing exit stream at the same place where, in 1897, Joseph Hunter and a crew of five hundred built his Golden River Dam, which held back the river water long enough for them to remove all the gold from the channel. Likely began as a construction work camp for this project, and its first name was Quesnelle Dam. When the community acquired a post office in 1923, it was renamed for John "Plato" Likely, one of the luckiest of the gold prospectors, who worked in the area during later gold-rush days. He received his moniker because of his great love of the Greek philosopher: he gave lectures on the subject from his lakeside camp under the cedars at today's Cedar Point Provincial Park. The highway bridge is a prime spot for watching spawning salmon in fall and the lake itself is famous for very large rainbow trout.

Early gold strikes in the area around Quesnel, Horsefly, and Cariboo Lakes were some of the richest. Before there was Barkerville or Richfield, and long before there was Likely, there were Cedar City, Keithley Creek, and Quesnelle Forks (this was the original spelling) and others, each with populations in the thousands. Miners spread out north over the Snowshoe Plateau and eventually arrived at Williams Creek for the richest strikes of all.

The village of Likely is a pleasant little settlement fringed by lawns on the river's edge. The Likely Hotel, a landmark for many years, still provides food and accommodation, and there is also a general store and a small gas station. Cedar Point Provincial Park (the site of old Cedar City), a short distance down the lake, displays mining machinery among its grove of old cedar trees. The park office (also a small museum) provides tourist information. Stop here to check conditions on the back road ahead, the wildest part of this adventure road.

You mustn't leave Likely without exploring BC's oldest, most complete, and best preserved ghost town: Quesnelle Forks. At the

Ghost Lake and the Falls, a short side trip.

confluence of the Quesnel and Cariboo Rivers, the town was once the largest of all the early gold-rush settlements, originally connected by a direct trail, a turnoff from the highway a few kilometres south of Likely. A bridge on this route washed out and has never been replaced, but the ghost town can be reached by another route, an unpaved twelve-kilometre road from Likely. Take Keithley Creek Road and watch for a left turn onto Rosette Lake Road. Be prepared for a rough drive over a forested ridge, then a steep drop to the river forks. Park just before the cemetery and explore the town on foot.

Begun in 1859 as a rough-and-ready miners' camp, it was surveyed as a townsite by the Royal Engineers in 1861. After a bridge was built, Quesnelle Forks soon became the largest settlement on the BC mainland. In its heyday, the town had twenty well-built log houses, a dozen stores, saloons, a Chinese tong house, government offices, two jail cells, and a cemetery. But it all came to an end after only two years. The new Wagon Road pushed through to Williams Creek, taking with it most of the goldfield traffic, and the town and the old trails began a swift decline. When spring floods washed away the river bridge Quesnelle Forks was almost abandoned.

Chinese inhabitants were the last to leave: they stayed behind to clean up the gold on the abandoned claims, establishing one of the first Chinese Canadian towns, with its own traditional, cultural, social, and spiritual traditions. With homes, shops and businesses, gardens, shrines, and a cemetery, it was the third-largest Chinatown in BC, just behind those of Victoria and Nanaimo. But eventually even the Chinese had to leave. The last lone occupant finally left in the 1950s. If the Chinese hadn't stayed on for so long, perhaps there would be nothing left of the town today.

A lonely ghost town lingered here on the river flats for years, its log buildings weathered a beautiful grey. But without preservation, ghost towns become ghostlier. And Quesnelle Forks is no different. Each year has seen more decline: roofs collapsed, log buildings burned, vandals attacked, spring freshets threatened the town's riverside frontage. The piles of shattered timbers increased. But this ghost town has survived. Named one of Canada's Historic Places in 2016, it is coming back to life. The old townsite has been surveyed, its buildings have been catalogued, and several have been restored. But don't expect a second Barkerville. Too much has been lost here, and the site is being restored as a ghost town. There is just enough left to get a sense of its past glory, to let your imagination take over, as the rivers roar and the wind whispers in the cottonwoods. Much of the work is being done here by volunteers from the Likely Historical Society and the Likely Cemetery Society, which keeps the graveyard in its immaculate state. There is a Forestry Recreation Site on the river bank and camping here is an ideal way to soak up the atmosphere. (For more information, or to give a donation, contact Quesnel Forks Restoration Project, Box 29, Likely, BC, V0L 1N0.)

The backroad to Barkerville starts out northeast from Likely on Keithley Creek Road, passes Paquette Lake, crosses the Cariboo River on a one-lane bridge, and continues on to a second river crossing, where a sign at the narrow wooden Bailey bridge reads "125 kilometres to Barkerville." The rest of the way, essentially a wilderness mountain route, mostly follows Forest Service Road 8400. But before you head across the bridge, continue on for a short distance upriver to Cariboo Lake and Keithley Creek, one of several gold-rush camps that pointed the way to Barkerville. One of the earliest communities, Keithley Creek started in July 1860 with a rich find by "Doc" Keithley in the creek that washes into the lake. Others miners soon crowded in to the rowdy camp, which optimists called Cariboo City, then started up the creek to find the motherlode. Once Doc had cleaned out his claim, he moved on to found another boomtown at Antler Creek, higher up in the hills, and this was superseded in turn by Lowhee Creek, Cameronton, and a host of others. Keithley Creek was perhaps the smallest of these flash-in-the-pan settlements, but it has survived, and it honours its history by looking after its tiny and very tidy graveyard. Outside the gates stands a small wooden shed, the Likely library, stocked with books of all kinds and unmanned. The door is not locked, and books can be borrowed free of charge or exchanged. Donations are welcome.

The original early gold rush trail that led from Keithley Creek over the Snowshoe Plateau is still here. But this is a difficult journey. Instead, backtrack to the river bridge and start an easier trek to Barkerville. The road follows the east shore of Cariboo Lake, but you won't see much of it because the forests are thick. However, if you are looking for a place to picnic, thirty-four kilometres from the bridge a short road leads down to the lake at Ladies Creek Recreation Site.

Mainline 8400 is the widest and most travelled road in this area, though it is easy to become confused by the number of side roads. There used to be a series of yellow signposts along the way, their mileage countdown starting both by the river bridge and at Barkerville, but in 2021 few of these remained. Make sure you keep on track: the 8400 signs are posted regularly. In 2021, at the only intersection where drivers were likely to go wrong, there was a hand-painted board pointing left to Barkerville. From here, the road climbs up to its highpoint on Cameron Ridge. When you reach the top, there's a surprise: A large brightly painted sign advertising

Barkerville, at last!

the Chocolate Moose Café at Cameron Ridge Bungalows. (Yes, they do serve chocolate mousse, and cheesecakes, too.) Customers park near the highway and take a short stroll up to a lookout point where the café and its outdoor wooden decks provide a wonderful view north across a little green valley to the mountains ahead. There are small cabins for rent, and trails lead up to Cameron Ridge and its flowery alpine meadows.

Around ninety kilometres from Likely there's a short side road you won't want to miss. It seems to head back the way you came and crosses boiling Matthew River before a right turn brings you to a small recreation site above Ghost Lake. A short trail from the parking lot leads down to a good, if precarious, view of the multi-stream Matthew River waterfalls.

On Google Maps, from here on Road 8400 is marked as the Matthew Valley Road. About five kilometres along at Comet Creek

Barkerville in tourist season.

there are yurt-like cabins built of stone—one used to be a restaurant. In 2021, these were not in use. The road winds its way south west and crosses the upper Cariboo River before turning north again toward the goldfields, passing another small recreation site, Whiskey Flats, beside Wolf Creek. From here it is only fourteen kilometres to Barkerville. At the junction with the Bowron Lakes Park Road, turn left for Highway 26 and Barkerville, your final destination, and spend the rest of the day reliving life in the most famous gold-rush town in BC. If you can, stay until most of the tourists and the actors go home. The empty main street will be full of shadows, full of old echoes, perhaps even full of spirits. By moonlight, the place will be extraordinary.

Best of all is Barkerville in the winter time, celebrating with the ghosts of Christmas past, or just silent under the snowdrifts. History really does come alive here. For one weekend in December the park is open, staffed, and merry. Horse-drawn sleigh rides through the snow, carol singing by lantern light, Christmas treats in the bakery, church services in beautiful old St. Saviour's—an amazing experience. Check barkerville.ca for information.

Most people would prefer to make this trip a circular adventure, returning to Quesnel and Highway 97 by way of Highway 26. If you do, make sure you take the short side road to Stanley, where all that remains is one old house and a large graveyard. And stop at the site of Blessing's grave to learn the story of his murder. Farther down the highway is one of the original roadhouses, Cottonwood House, now a provincial historic site. Another worthwhile place to explore.

8. HEARTLANDS OF THE GITXSAN
THE TOTEM VILLAGES ALONG THE SKEENA

In the forested heartlands along the Skeena and Bulkley Rivers, history is long and enduring, recorded on village totems of the Gitxsan, the ancestral First Nations people. Carved here are the myths and traditions of an ancient society, with its own laws and world views, and its own very deep roots. Today we can visit these historic villages with their collections of very old totem poles and enjoy the magical misty landscape around them—but not without a feeling of unease. Two cultures collided here, and one of them, the most ancient, was badly damaged.

The rich lands of the Gitxsan (People of the River Mist) remained remote and mostly untouched until quite late in the written history of BC. While a few fur traders and missionaries penetrated the mountains, and items such as iron pots, blankets, and guns were in early use, acquired at the coast from early Spanish and English sailing expeditions, the people had little direct contact with Europeans until the 1860s. By then the Collins Overland Telegraph Line was being stretched across the country to connect North

OPPOSITE A fisherman braves the mists of dawn below the Bulkley Canyon.

Last light at Kitwancool.

America to Europe via Alaska's Bering Strait. Paddlewheelers came up the Skeena from the coast with surveyors, supplies, and manpower. The project brought strange things into the country: huge caches of wire, gangs of loggers and linemen, boozy shantytowns—and, unhappily, catastrophic European diseases, which killed large numbers of Indigenous people.

The telegraph scheme fizzled out—a competitor successfully laid a cable beneath the Atlantic—but a gate to the outside world had been opened. Up the rivers and along the trails came foreigners to clear the land, build homes, and start farms. Next to the site of the Indigenous village of Gitanmaax, the pioneer steamboat settlement of Hazelton at the junction of the Skeena and Bulkley Rivers became an important point of departure for the Omineca gold rush of 1869–73. The Gitxsan way of life, intact for thousands of years, was utterly changed—but by no means extinguished.

This adventure road begins at the great canyon of the Bulkley River on Highway 16, about thirty kilometres east of Hazelton. Here the river boils through a deep and narrow rock slot, one of the very best places to watch Indigenous fishermen at work. With security ropes tied around their waists, they stand daringly on the edge of the rocks, in the full spray of the foaming river, fishing with long dip nets. In fall, when the salmon are running, both sides of the canyon are lined with fishermen, and there are usually just as many spectators, watching from the highway pull-off or from the bridge at the canyon neck. The noise of the river thundering through the gap is deafening, and the silver gleam of leaping salmon is one of the world's great sights. The river has a mesmerizing effect,

Fishing the traditional way in the Bulkley Canyon.

and time passes swiftly. But spare a few minutes to visit the museum, high above the canyon, and to explore the village of Moricetown, named for Oblate missionary Father Adrien-Gabriel Morice. The church of Our Lady of the Rosary was built in 1912, but the village is far older. Its original name is Kyah Wiget, which translates as "old village," an appropriate name since archaeological excavations here have found signs of habitation dating back at least four thousand years.

    Follow the Bulkley River west along the highway to where it joins the larger Skeena River, a historic nexus for the Indigenous people of the area and the end of safe navigation for paddlewheelers coming up from the coast. Call in at the New Hazelton Visitor Centre, a neat log cabin beside Highway 16, for a useful brochure detailing an auto route through the area where informational plaques at historic sites are heralded by large Hands of History signs (an open hand is a Gitxsan sign of peace). Highway 62 nearby leads to Old Hazelton and the ancestral lands of the Gitxsan Nation.

Skeena River and the Roche de Boule Mountains.

To get there, the highway crosses the Bulkley River as it roars through the narrow, winding Hagwilget Canyon. The bridge itself is an adventure in engineering: a one-way road suspended on a steel spider web high above the river. There are generous parking spaces beside the highway here because most visitors want to walk across. The view from the bridge is heady and exciting, the canyon deep and curvaceous, the tumbling waters a bright, glacial green.

This bridge was built in 1931, but there has been a crossing here for centuries. Archival photos show earlier versions as frail, twiggy affairs of cedar poles lashed together, first with roots, then later with wire left behind from the telegraph fiasco. The Indigenous village at Hagwilget (Tse-kya), across the bridge to the right, is known for the 1908 Church of St. Mary Magdalene, with its unique sunburst bullseye window and many pinnacled spire—but sometimes the canyon gets all the attention.

Before this trip goes any farther into the Gitxsan world, make a stop at the old pioneer town of Hazelton, where Highway 62 ends. (At less

OPPOSITE, TOP Reconstructed Gitxan village. 'Ksan is the Indigenous name for the Skeena River.

BOTTOM Old totems rest outside 'Ksan carvers shed.

HEARTLANDS OF THE GITXSAN: THE TOTEM VILLAGES ALONG THE SKEENA 155

ABOVE One of the many totems at 'Ksan.

OPPOSITE View from the bridge: Hagwilget Canyon.

than eight kilometres long, this highway must be one of the shortest in BC.) Drive past the Kispiox Valley Road and enter the Victorian world of a riverboat town started in 1866 around the HBC trading post and surveyed into townsite lots by Edgar Dewdney in 1871. In its glory years, as a supplier of everything needed for the telegraph line, the gold rush of the Omineca, and the great influx of homesteaders and entrepreneurs, the little settlement boomed. It was the centre of everything, supplied by a fleet of steamboats from Prince Rupert. But destiny was against it.

It was bypassed in 1914 by the Great Northern Railway, later by Highway 16, and replaced in importance by a new community, known as New Hazelton, which sits alongside today's highway. Old Hazelton, however, has more charisma than its upstart rival, and tourists love it. It is a quiet place and there is much to see: more than twenty-five late-nineteenth-century buildings can be seen here, including St. Peter's Anglican Church, prominent along the riverside walk. And right beside the town, in the arms of the two rivers, is the Gitxsan Historical Village of 'Ksan, where one can experience far older histories.

While it is a reconstruction, everything about 'Ksan is authentic, even the site: it has been occupied for at least seven thousand years.

Church of St. Mary Magdalene at Tse-kya, village near the canyon.

On a wide meadow, a large semicircle of longhouses built of red cedar are painted with spirited tribal motifs. The first house is the entrance/gift shop where one can arrange tours of the living museums inside the Fireweed, Eagle, and Wolf houses, where ceremonies, including the traditional potlatch are still held. Most of the traditional clothing and regalia on display is worn by members of the 'Ksan Performing Arts Group, which usually puts on shows in the Wolf House in July and August. The Frog house used to host a school where Gitxsan traditions of wood carving were handed down to new generations. The school is currently closed, but totems and other items are still being made here. In the late summer of 2021, Dan Yunkws was busy carving a huge cedar pole for a school in Smithers. The totem poles in front of the houses commemorate the four Gitxsan clans. But one of the poles, raised for the village opening in 1970, sports a most untraditional motif: a man wearing a top hat and bow tie, said to be W.A.C. Bennett, BC's premier at the time.

Walk through the meadow to the traditional grave house, and continue down to the river's edge for an outstanding view of the mountain known as Stii Kyo Din ("stands alone"), called Rocher Déboule ("mountain of rolling stones") by the first Europeans to come here. Both the Bulkley and the Skeena are prime salmon streams.

The Kispiox Valley Road into the Gitxsan villages starts a short distance back along Highway 24: turn left (north) at the gas station.

Totems at Kispiox.

The road follows the Skeena River on its winding path, crossing it twice on one-way wooden bridges. After the first bridge, five kilometres along, a turning leads to Glen Vowell (Sik-E-Dakh), a relatively new village (no totem poles), where the Salvation Army built an elaborate citadel in 1900.

Immediately after a second bridge, near the confluence with the Kispiox River, is the village of Anspayaxw, "the hiding place." On most maps it's still called Kispiox or "loud talkers," a name given to the village by one of the first Indian agents. The community is large, and there are about fifteen hereditary poles set up for display near the riverbank—there are signs to lead the way. These works of art are magnificent symbols of the society's history, pride, and culture, a glimpse into an ancient world of myth and legend. Some date from the 1880s, while others are more recent. They were raised for several reasons: to honour the dead, proclaim ownership, record encounters with the supernatural, or to commemorate events in Gitxsan history.

Peeping behind the totems is the 1949 Pierce Memorial United Church, which has an interesting three-tiered tower decorated with

Totem detail, still with traces of paint, Kitwanga.

pinnacles. It was named after the Tsimshian-Scottish pastor who came here in 1895 and stayed for fifteen years.

If you are interested in learning about the totems, enquire at the nearby cultural/administrative office, a cedar building decorated with traditional motifs and flanked by two poles carved in 1976 by the esteemed artist Walter Harris. You can hire guides here for cultural tours as well as hiking, fly-fishing, and river-float trips.

Kispiox (or Anspayaxw) also holds the final strands of a piece of non-Indigenous history: it's the site of Fort Stager, where the ill-fated Collins Overland Telegraph Line came to an abrupt stop. (The fort was built as an administrative and supply depot, not for defence.) The line had been strung eight hundred kilometres north, from New Westminster to Quesnel, then west to Hazelton and north again, heading for Alaska and the Bering Strait. It was already forty

Totem detail.

kilometres up the Kispiox River before word came, in August 1866, that the race was lost. Further construction was halted, though the telegraph office at Fort Stager continued to operate for the next three years before closing down for good.

The adventure road doubles back through the valley to Highway 16 and follows the Skeena west for forty kilometres. There is much to see in this land of the Gitxsan. About ten kilometres from New Hazleton is Seeley Lake Provincial Park, a swimming and fishing hole with a pleasant campsite. The park is well worth a stop, if only to ponder an interesting local legend that describes how Medeek, an enormous grizzly bear, once roared up out of the lake, ripping up local mountains and destroying villages—a harsh punishment for the people who had insulted the trout spirits by using their bones as ornaments. The tale has been told for a long, long time and perhaps it was not just make-believe. In the 1980s, geologists found traces here of a three-thousand-year-old "great ecological upheaval," when the greater part of the mountain collapsed and caused a devastating flood. Another place nearby is the source of a similar legend. On the opposite side of the Skeena is the mythical site of Txemlax'amid, where all the people of the area were thought to have once lived together in peace. Children tormenting a baby goat incurred the wrath of the mountain goat spirit, who punished the community by summoning a devastating landslide. Perhaps the two old tales are simply different versions of the same event.

The village of Gitsegukla, about twenty-six kilometres along the highway west of Hazelton, has a venerable triple-towered church (built in 1930), and a big new school, decorated inside and out with traditional designs of Grouse, Frog, Wolf, Owl, and Killer Whale. There is even a carving of Medeek. The village holds a special place in Gitxsan history. In 1872, while all the villagers were away fishing, a mining prospector's out-of-control camp fire accidentally destroyed all the village poles and canoes. The people of Gitsegukla appealed in vain for compensation, then took matters into their own hands. They blockaded the Skeena, holding up vital boat traffic, and trade and commerce upstream came to a halt until the BC government met their demands.

Sixteen kilometres west, the Stewart–Cassiar Highway 37, finished in 1972, shoots north on its seven hundred-kilometre journey to Yukon. This paved road through the valley of the Kitwanga River follows the route of the ancient Grease Trail that linked the Gitxsan villages with the eulachon fisheries on the Nass River, far to the north. Similar in looks and size to smelt, eulachon was much valued for its oil, which stayed fresh and could be stored and traded. It was also known as the candlefish because, when dried and set alight, it would burn brightly like a candle.

The village of Gitwangak (marked as Kitwanga on most maps) lies beside the Grease Trail just north of Highway 37's bridge across the Skeena River. To reach the totems, turn right on Bridge Street immediately past the bridge, stopping to mourn the loss of the historic 1893 St. Paul's Church, which went up in flames in 2021. Its four hundred-year-old stained glass windows, sent from England, and elegant steeple are gone, but the adjacent bell tower, with its elaborate wooden "embroidery" patterns, fortunately stood far enough away to escape the flames. The bell tower was built in 1979, when the church was restored.

Gitwangak means "people of the place of rabbits," though the three village clans are Eagle, Wolf and Frog, all finely represented on the village totem poles that stand beside the river. Allow some time here to admire the workmanship and the lovely worn patina of these ancient monuments. Follow the road through the newer part of the village, reconnect with Highway 37, and continue northeast through the Kitwanga River valley.

Watch for a loop road (about seven kilometres from Highway 16) signposted to Gitwangak Battle Hill National Historic Site. From the roadside parking lot look down into the valley to see the site of a Gitxsan ta'awdzep, or fortress, known locally as Battle Hill, a rounded hump some thirteen metres high. The top of this hill was once protected by a palisade and ringed by a great stack of huge logs that could be rolled down to crush invaders. Inside the palisade were communal houses, with food pits and trapdoors that led to secret escape routes. Of these, nothing remains today.

This totem at Kitwanga, called Hole in the Sky, is a replica. The original, featured in a painting by Emily Carr, is in the Royal BC Museum.

According to Gitxsan oral history, this hill fort belonged to the great warrior 'Nekt. The son of a Haida chief and a Kispiox woman, as a baby, 'Nekt had been carried off to Haida Gwaii during a raid. His mother raced after him, killed his father, cut off his head, and took it with her as she escaped with her infant son, home across the ocean in a canoe. This event is pictured on one of the totem poles in Gitwangak. You can look for it on your return journey. According to the legend, when the baby cried, his mother cut out the chief's tongue and gave it to 'Nekt as a soother.

'Nekt grew up to become a fierce warrior who protected himself in battle with the skin of a grizzly bear lined with pitch and sheets of slate. In this armour, and brandishing his magic war club, he was believed to be invincible. From the hilltop fortress here he led many successful raids to coastal settlements, where he was mistaken for a magic spirit bear. But in his last great battle, fought here in the early 1800s, 'Nekt was killed, his armour pierced by a bullet, reputedly from the first musket ever fired along the Skeena.

Is there any truth to this story? Archaeologists investigated the site in 1979, and while they have no proof that 'Nekt ever existed, they did find evidence of the palisade, five communal houses, and a large number of pits, some of which could have been linked to underground escape routes. Tree ring and charcoal dating established that the hilltop settlement had been in use for more than a hundred years and that the site burned in the 1830s, when the first guns arrived in trade from the coast.

Feast your eyes on the view from the parking lot down to this historic fortress park by the Kitwanga River. The hill is a natural formation, probably of glacial origin. In summer green, it glows like an emerald. A very long flight of steps leads down from the highway to a marked trail leading around the hill and up to the summit. Nothing at all remains of the fortifications, but keep the story in your head and it will all come to life. There are Parks Canada informative signs along the trail, in English, French, and Gitxsanmx.

The road from the fort continues north to rejoin Highway 37. About ten kilometres farther along, take Kitwanga Access Road which angles left to the village of Gitanyow. This was its original name, meaning "place of many people." After warfare and disease reduced its numbers, it changed its name to Kitwancool, "people of a small village." Today, population growth has made its first name far more appropriate: Gitanyow is a large village, the only Gitxsan settlement not alongside the Skeena River.

Until 1950, the village was isolated, accessible only by the Grease Trail, and this helped to preserve the totems, twenty-two of which are still standing. Because of the number of poles, their age (mid- to late nineteenth century), and their position in a grassy meadow, the village was declared a Canadian Historic Site in 1972. Three of the oldest and frailest poles, including the 140-year-old "Hole in the Sky" pole made famous by painter Emily Carr, are in the Royal Provincial Museum in Victoria for preservation, and replicas, made by Kwakwaka̱'wa̱kw carver Henry Hunt, were erected in their place. Emily Carr travelled to the Skeena by wagon in 1928 to capture what she believed was a vanishing art form. She was wrong: new poles are being carved and old ones restored in First Nations villages throughout BC.

The Gitanyow totems are a national treasure. To reach the site on First Avenue, take the first main road on the right, which curves around the eastern edge of the village. All are wonderfully different, many topped by birds and animals. Allow plenty of time to study them all. Many have been restored and are supported by metal braces. There is a large interpretive centre nearby (check at the village office for information about opening hours) and a carving shed, built in the style of a longhouse.

Highway 37 continues north to Yukon, and at Cranberry Junction, about fifty kilometres north of Gitanyow, a back road leads west up the Cranberry River to New Aiyansh (Gitlaxt'aamiks) in the valley of the Nass River. This unpaved route, a continuation of Highway 113, provides a gravel shortcut between this adventure road and the one that explores the land of the Nisga̱'a. Check the road and weather conditions before you attempt this.

To call it a day, return south to Highway 16, checking in at Gitwangak on your way to see the 'Nekt story pole (canoe, baby, mother and, yes, even the tongue) and continue east or west, depending on your overnight destination.

9. TRACKING AN OLD MURDER THROUGH THE NICOLA HILLS

Some journeys follow, as best they can, the explorations of the great men of history: Alexander Mackenzie's overland trail to the Pacific; Peter Fidler's first crossing, north to south, of today's Alberta (both, coincidentally, in 1793); or farther afield, Hannibal's trek, with a huge army and thirty-nine elephants, across the Alps in 218 BC. This journey also follows a historic route, but one far less epic in scope. It revisits the scene of a horrific nineteenth-century murder of a police constable by a gang of very young horse thieves, the three McLean brothers and their friend, and tracks their escape route through the hills and valleys of the Nicola Country.

It is an adventure road for certain, but there is much to ponder here, as you follow the dramatic saga. Could a fairly routine theft of a horse have spiralled into murder if the McLean boys had not been outsiders? They were of mixed race: their father, Donald, an ex-HBC factor, had been killed in the Chilcotin War by warring First Nations; their mother, Sophia, an Indigenous woman from the Cache Creek area, was shunned by both her own people and the settlers. When a small government compensation payment for her husband's death ran out,

OPPOSITE From the high murder scene, Manning Road winds down to meet the Kamloops Highway.

A huge stack of hay bales marks the gate to the Ussher Monument.

the family was destitute. The boys ran wild. Caught in the clash between cultures, the boys did not belong anywhere. They had nowhere to go.

The tale begins in Kamloops in 1879. The bad guys are brothers Allan, Charlie, and Archie McLean and their friend Alex Hare, teenagers with a long record of cattle rustling, theft, and general hell-raising. The good guys are John Tannatt Ussher, constable and government agent, two ranchers, William Palmer and John McLeod, and Amni Shumway, a Mormon freighter and tracker.

The story: It was December 7, with deep snow shrouding the hills. The boys had been in Kamloops jail for horse theft and highway robbery but escaped (as they had done several times before) and took to the hills. That day, rancher William Palmer notices that his best stallion was missing and rides up onto Long Lake range to look for him. He sees the McLean boys with his horse, but being alone, he fears confrontation, and so after a brief chat with them, he rides back to Kamloops. Constable Ussher gathers together a posse, appointing Palmer, McLeod, and Shumway as special constables, and a reward of $250 is offered for the boys' capture.

It is late afternoon. The snow is falling and the group rides out quickly, hoping to find the trail before dark. They pass the cabin of John McLeod, who agrees to join them, and they all stay for the night at the horse camp where William Roxborough is wintering the horses of the CP railway crew. In the bitter cold of dawn on December 8 they follow faint tracks south toward the hump of Brigade Hill. Horses are spotted near a small campfire in a clearing surrounded by aspen and young firs; the lawmen move close. The outlaw boys, hidden behind the trees, raise their rifles. A gunshot misses Palmer but grazes McLeod on the cheek. He fires back, but his borrowed shotgun falters and he takes another bullet, this time in the knee. His horse is also peppered with shot.

This rock cairn is a monument to Johnny Ussher at the scene of his murder.

Into the melee strides Constable Ussher. He knows these boys well. He jumps off his horse, leaving his gun on the saddle, and pleads with them to surrender. He reaches out to Hare, but Hare stabs him and he falls. Archie McLean puts a gun to the side of the constable's head and fires. Ussher lies crumpled on the blood-stained snow and Hare keeps stabbing.

Gunfire continues. In all, thirty shots are fired. With one dead and one badly injured man to care for, the posse rides back to Kamloops for reinforcements. The outlaws strip the dead man of his coat, boots, and gloves and ride off with his horse and gun, heading south to Douglas Lake. They come across shepherd Jim Kelly, sitting on a rock, playing his mouth organ near his cabin at the north end of Stump Lake. Another altercation, another murder. They take Kelly's pistol, prized watch, and mouth organ, and continue south, stopping

TRACKING AN OLD MURDER THROUGH THE NICOLA HILLS 169

Brigade Lake, where the HBC fur brigade camped along the route of the fugitives, is also on maps as Long Lake.

by several settlers' cabins to commandeer guns and ammunition as they head for the Indigenous village of Spaxomin on Douglas Lake.

The McLean boys, being half-Indigenous, hope that the villagers will come to their aid, but Chief Chillihitzia is adamantly opposed to helping them, even though Allan is married to one of his daughters, Angele. The boys hole up in an old cabin near the Nicola River, where, after a four-day siege, they surrender. Their journey ends, a year or so later, at the New Westminster gallows.

The adventure road that follows the Wild McLean boys on their journey of murder and mayhem begins at Long Lake Road, a turning off Highway 5A, south of Kamloops, the old road to Merritt. Once it leaves the cluster of houses and mail boxes at Knutsford, the road, then one of the HBC brigade trails south, is the most likely route for the fugitives to take. It is still remarkably rural, mostly still rangeland, a beautiful mix of shady forest and grassland, an area the boys probably knew well. Side roads provide invitations to Goose and Edith Lakes, but keep straight to cross Anderson Creek, which is roughly where Shumway first picked up the outlaws' tracks. About nine kilometres from Knutsford, the large blue lake glimpsed through the trees on the

A fine old log barn near the turnoff to Brigade Lake.

west wide of the road has been named for John McLeod; the low hill opposite for Amni Shumway, the tracker.

To really slip back into the times it should be winter, bruisingly cold and with blowing snow. It is difficult to resurrect the mood of that sombre day when summer's wild roses and lupines bloom riotously along the road edges, or fall scatters golden showers of aspen leaves. But the McLean Boys did come this way, turning east (about fourteen kilometres from Knutsford) near the junction with Jackson Road to their night camp. The brigade route carried straight on to the lake known as both Long Lake and Brigade Lake. Just three kilometres from the intersection, the lake is a sinuous ripple of blue tucked into the folds of grassy hills. It was a perfect spot for the brigade's three hundred packhorses and men to feed and rest. Today, it's a great place for birders, a great place for a picnic, and a great place to take photos: there's an old homestead on the far side of the lake for a focal point.

To reach the McLeans' camp, the murder scene, return to Jackson Road, drive east for about six hundred metres, then turn south down Manning Road to a group of old corrals and a stack of round hay bales. Park here, walk through the gate (remembering to close it afterwards), and follow a rough track southeast to a small pond. Circle

The high, rolling grassland of the Nicola Valley was the end of the road for the killers of Constable Ussher.

around this to a small clearing in the trees, just to the east. In the centre, a stark pyramid of granite rocks marks the site where Ussher died. An inscribed plaque remembers the lawman who "unarmed and fearless [...] gave his life to secure peace and order in our growing west." A lake named after Ussher lies in the trees to the east. It is a sombre place, and it is easy to re-enact the murder scene, even in the summer, with the wind clattering in the trees and the grass more brown than green. In spring, wildflowers—shooting stars, pink avens, and violets—bloom in memoriam.

After the killing, the McLeans and Hare rode south along the Brigade Trail, which heads down to the valley floor at Napier Lake, where it meets today's highway. This part of their flight route is hard to locate, and it is better today to return to Jackson Road and follow it to the highway, though in a slow and meandering way, more north than east. Little travelled, this road is gravel and narrow in places.

Highway 5A, once the main road between Kamloops and Princeton, has been supplanted, north of Merritt, by the Coquihalla Highway, Highway 5, which slashes through the landscape from Hope to Kamloops. Luckily the old road has been left as a modest two-lane road, a far more interesting route since it follows the contours of the land, a narrow glaciated valley with a string of long lakes, and still bears many relics of pioneer days. This was the road the McLean boys followed.

Names of the men in the posse are everywhere: Campbell Creek Road, just north of Shumway Lake, leads into another scenic valley where John McLeod moved in 1881. Amni Shumway homesteaded on the lake now named after him, its sides so steep that the road rides high above its western flanks. South lies Trapp Lake, where rancher Thomas Trapp was visited by the outlaws (they took his money and guns, but not his life), and then Napier Lake and Stump Lake. Here Jim Kelly, always antagonistic toward the young hoodlums, was killed. The outlaws then took off down the old Kamloops Road which veers off to the east here, beside historic Stump Lake Ranch, and rejoins the highway a few kilometres south.

The fur traders pioneered this route away from the lake because its well-watered meadows provided better grazing for their animals. At a viewpoint along this unpaved detour, a sign verifies that this is indeed an HBC historic route. The old road is rough and narrow, and you might choose to keep to the main highway instead.

Nicola Lake is the largest in this string of valley lakes and lies just a few kilometres south. When French-Canadian fur traders came through the area in the 1800s, they knew it all as Nicola's Country, named for a famous chief of the Spaxomin Nation whose proper name, Hwistesmetxē'qen, or "Walking Grizzly Bear," they found too difficult to pronounce. The traders called him simply Nicholas, or Nkwala, and the river became known as Nicola's River. John Tod, chief trader at Fort Kamloops, described Nkwala as "a great chieftain and a bold man for he had 17 wives." He fathered more

FOLLOWING SPREAD The route from Kamloops to Merritt follows a string of lakes, where the first settlers staked their land.

Old Highway 5, south of Kamloops.

than fifty children and was known as a peacemaker, both between different Indigenous Peoples and between the First Nations and the newcomers: the fur traders, miners, and ranchers. The highway follows the outlaws' journey along the east side of this great lake and soon arrives at Douglas Lake Road by the Indigenous village of Quilchena, with its strikingly modern log church. Here the boys turned east toward the village of Spaxomin.

But before taking this road, continue south a short distance to visit one of BC's historic treasures, the Quilchena Hotel, which sits beside the lake. This magnificent hostelry continues the traditions of Edwardian gentility that began in 1908, when rancher Joseph Guichon, firmly believing that the CPR would route its new line from Merritt through the Nicola Valley, built this huge three-storey building to accommodate future railway passengers. But the CPR had other plans and Quilchena's hopes were dashed. Still, it soldiered on, keeping alive the traditions of the British Empire: polo matches, fishing derbies, fancy dress balls, and five-course dinners. Despite the best of efforts, the hotel was forced to close in 1917 after only nine years of operation, but all the old furnishings and fixtures were kept intact by the family.

The HBC Brigade route is now unpaved Old Kamloops Road.

When the hotel reopened in 1958, it offered a snapshot of times past: guests could still sleep in the Ladies' Parlour or the bridal suite, socialize over tea in a period drawing room, and exercise elbows in the ornate bar (look for the bullet holes and ask for the story behind them). Today, while it retains much of its original ambience, the hotel has been thoroughly modernized. Open only during the summer months, it was forced to close because of the COVID-19 pandemic. At time of writing there were plans to reopen in 2022, but offering a different, more exclusive kind of experience. Adjacent to the hotel is a gas station and an old-time general store where blue jeans, fancy buckles, and Stetsons share the shelves with groceries and videos.

Douglas Lake Road, just north of Quilchena, follows the valley of the Nicola River and a string of lakes through a very scenic grassland slice of the Interior Plateau. It is one of the very best of BC's country roads: nothing much has changed here since the land was settled back in the 1800s. At the south end of Douglas Lake, about fifteen kilometres from the highway, the Indigenous village of Spaxomin witnessed the final episode of the McLeans' sad story.

ABOVE This Nicola barn, beside Highway 5, is close to the shoot-out scene.
OPPOSITE St. Nicholas at Spaxomin was once in the centre of the village.

After being refused sanctuary by Chief Chillinetza the gang holed up in a small cabin built from cottonwood logs fairly close to the river. They arrived on December 9. They had food, some wood for the fire, and whisky—but only a little water in a bucket. As the days wore on, they became very much aware that they were surrounded—outside, sixty men were watching and waiting, working in shifts in the bitter cold. Archie made the first move, shooting and wounding one of the ranchers. A message was delivered, ordering them to surrender. The boys stayed put and soon ran out of water: several attempts to get to the river and back failed amid a volley of gunshots. There was no escape. After four days, the boys, chilled to the bone and hungry, surrendered. They were shackled and taken back to Kamloops to be charged for their crimes then sent to the security of the jail in New Westminster where they would be put on trial.

Their travel in the dead of an exceedingly bitter winter was slow and laborious. They left Kamloops on December 17. It took them a day to reach Cache Creek, four days to reach Chilliwack, along

A cowboy outside the store at Quilchena.

the Cariboo Road, and another three to get to New Westminster jail, arriving there on Christmas day. No plum pudding awaited them. After a long and complicated trial, all four were found guilty of murder and later hanged.

In a way it seems wrong to tell this macabre story in the idyllic grassland setting of the Nicola Valley. So, to switch the mood to more peaceful adventures, with no ugly strings attached, continue into the lovely landscape alongside Douglas Lake to the ranch itself. Access to the lake is limited except at Prince Philip Point, named to commemorate the royal visit of 1962 and a good place for birdwatching. Keep a lookout for osprey along the lake: they nest on platforms specially built to discourage them from using the power-line poles. At the northeastern end of the lake, the road right-angles to bridge the Nicola River and heads through meadows toward the village of Douglas Lake, headquarters for the sprawling ranch operations. There's a general store here, and the old Woodward's Department Store delivery truck is a reminder that this gigantic ranch was once owned by the Woodward family.

Farther along, the serene waters of a small lake known as The Sanctuary, create mirror images of the red-roofed ranch buildings as the road bypasses the village, crests a small hill, and runs beside the ranch airstrip. Once past the bullpens and the feedlots, it curves

Douglas Lake Ranch headquarters.

around to cross the Nicola River again beside a cluster of corrals and a great old log barn at English Bridge. From here, the road strikes northeast to touch the end of sprawling Chapperon Lake.

It was somewhere near here that the final stage of another turn-of-the-century crime took place. Bill Miner, a "gentleman bandit" who, according to legend, introduced the expression "hands up" and never killed anyone, held up and robbed a CPR train near the station of Ducks, east of Kamloops. On their getaway run, he and his two accomplices camped near the lake, where they were captured peacefully by a Mounted Police posse. Miner was tried, found guilty, and imprisoned in, and later escaped from, the New Westminster jail. One version of his story was told in the movie *The Grey Fox*.

Chapperon Lake, headquarters for Douglas Lake's eastern operations, seems to mark the end of the open grasslands: the road dives briefly into forest for its journey past Rush Lake, shallow and reedy, noisy with bird life, and over the divide into the Salmon River drainage. Salmon Lake is home to a popular fishing camp, its string of small cabins spaced along the shore. The resort office has basic snacks, coffee, and information. Just past the lake, stop to admire a fine hewn-log house, long deserted but inhabited today by a family of yellow-bellied marmots.

The Salmon River has a long way to go before it reaches its destination: Shuswap Lake, near the town of Salmon Arm. As it races north, down from the high grasslands and into the forest, it carves a narrow canyon through volcanic rocks, a source of agate for local rockhounds. Its narrow valley then opens up into riverside farmland. At the junction with Highway 97, the old settlement of Westwold has a general store and a couple of cafés. From here there are three options: you can go south to Vernon, passing pioneer St. Luke's Church, built in 1898, north to Kamloops, or take the Salmon River Road all the way to Shuswap Lake.

OPPOSITE A sturdy log house on the Douglas Lake Road.

10. | CHILCOTIN
THE LONG AND LONELY ROAD TO THE SEA

Highway 20 is one of only three main roads that link BC's heartland to the sea, and of the three it is the loneliest. It begins its 450-kilometre journey at the intersection with Highway 97 at the south end of Williams Lake, traverses dry, open rangeland, climbs over a high pass in the Coast Mountains, and then plunges down into the Great Bear Rainforest, at the head of North Bentinck Arm. The road ends at the tiny town of Bella Coola, which is still one hundred kilometres from the open ocean, protected by the great maze of fiord-like inlets and islands that line the outer coast. It is an adventure of geographic contrasts, and the road's grand finale, a steep descent from subalpine to coastal rainforest, will be long remembered.

Chilcotin Country, west of the Fraser River, is huge, sprawling, and wild. The road through it traces only a very narrow corridor, giving you just a taste of this lonely land. West of Williams Lake, near Doc English Bluff, a huge limestone outcrop laid down in tropical

OPPOSITE Hoodoos rise in tall, spectacular clusters.

FOLLOWING SPREAD This bridge over the Fraser River, west of Williams Lake, is the unofficial divide between the Cariboo and the Chilcotin.

Chilcotin Lodge provides old-fashioned comfort.

the river a beautiful icy blue-green, the landscape tawny shades of gold and green. A bridge crosses the river here, and a winding road provides access. You must make time for this detour.

The road starts easily enough, cutting across a long stretch of natural grassland that slopes gradually down toward the river. Just before the start of the switchbacks leading down to the canyon, a small rest area provides trailhead access to Junction Sheep Range Provincial Park, wild land set aside in the wedge of hills between the Chilcotin and the Fraser Rivers to protect the largest herd of California bighorn sheep in North America, a species in decline. There are no park facilities here, just wide open spaces, great views, and a chance to see the sheep and other wildlife.

The sheep don't stay in the park, of course. They also forage right around the road as it begins its steep and circuitous descent—a whole series of hairpin bends—to the bridge in the narrowest part of the river canyon. The bridge here is an old one, made of wood and barely wide enough for the loaded logging trucks that sometimes thunder across it, raising great clouds of dust along the road. The surging river has carved deeply through vast deposits of yellow-grey glacial

ABOVE The long switchback road down to Farwell Canyon.

BELOW The Chilcotin River swirls around the hoodoos at Farwell Canyon.

silt and clay, and wind and rain have worked the sediments into spectacular formations: serrated towers and tapering pinnacles thrust up from the steep talus slopes. The Tŝilhqot'in name for the canyon is Nagwentled, or "place of landslides"—a most appropriate choice.

Protected mountain sheep range in the hills.

This beautiful area will tempt you to linger. There are several parking spots, good viewpoints, and hiking trails—one to huge "walking" sand dunes, and another leading from a meadow viewpoint right down to a bench on the river's edge, where there used to be a small ranch. A few old cabins remain here, and there are informal camping spots under the willows. The bridge area is a traditional Tŝilhqot'in steelhead and salmon fishing site. The forestry road across the bridge will lead, eventually, into the lands of the Gang Ranch and to the Churn Creek Bridge across the Fraser. (See page 58.)

Returning to the Chilcotin Highway, the road passes a ranch with a large red-roofed barn, all that remains of the once famous Becher House, built in 1892. For many years this historic and luxurious roadhouse was an outpost oasis of European culture. It had the first telephone in the Chilcotin, the first automobile (a Cadillac)—and the only saloon in the area. The original house burned in 1915; the second, even more luxurious, kept going until the 1940s, when the highway passed it by. A ghostly derelict by 1981, it was finally demolished that same year.

Taking its place on the highway just west of the intersection the fine old two-storey Chilcotin Lodge has provided good food and accommodation since the 1940s. One couldn't wish for a better, more authentic place to stay. The log lodge has an old-fashioned feel: its guest lounge has a huge stone fireplace and comfy sofas, there is a billiard room, loads of books, and cozy bedrooms upstairs. It's the perfect place to slip into the right frame of mind for a Chilcotin adventure.

ABOVE View of the Chilcotin River and some of the burnt forests.

OPPOSITE This totem outside Anaham Gas Station was made in Bella Coola.

Continuing west, the hills around Becher's Pond Recreation Site and in patches all along the eastern part of the highway have suffered much from forest fires—the black spikes of burnt trees are reminders of several seasons when the Cariboo-Chilcotin was up in flames. It wasn't only trees that were burned, though. The little historic store, post office, and café at Lee's Corner, near the community of Hanceville, about fifty kilometres farther along, also went up in flames. The business was named for pioneer Norman Lee, the

FOLLOWING SPREAD A storm over the Chilcotin plateau in its fall glory.

Old log cabins and a split rail fence—a typical Chilcotin scene.

first non-Indigenous rancher in the area, who became famous for his brave but calamitous attempt in 1898 to drive a herd of two hundred cattle north through the wilderness to Dawson City in Yukon, a trek of 2,500 kilometres. His book *Klondike Cattle Drive* tells the story. The nearby community of Hanceville was named for another pioneer, Tom Hance, who set up the original trading post here in 1875. The Hanceville Cut-Off Road at the old "corner" continues southwest across the Chilcotin River into one of the loneliest and loveliest parts of the plateau, the Nemaiah Valley. The river bridge, just five kilometres down from the highway, makes a great picnic stop.

There are several small communities west of Lee's Corner. The first is Anaham (Tl'etinqox), which has a gas station (with a coastal totem outside, carved in Bella Coola), and the architecturally amazing log church of the Sacred Heart of Jesus. Farther along, as the highway comes closer to the river, is Alexis Creek, which also has a church, St. Luke's, and a large old general store. Across the road here from the historic Chilcotin Hotel (presently closed) there's a tidy little visitor centre. Bird lovers will know that a road north from the village leads to Stum Lake Provincial Park, the only BC nesting grounds of the white pelicans, and often closed to protect the nests.

At Bull Canyon just to the west, the highway comes close to the Chilcotin River, boiling to a frenzy as it dashes between the high rock walls. There is a campsite here, and a short trail leads along the river's edge. This interesting little spot was once used for bull containment, as its name suggests. Just a few kilometres up from the canyon, on a bench still known locally as Hudson's Bay Flats, the HBC built their (unsuccessful) fur-trading post of Fort Chilcotin in the 1830s. There is nothing left of it now, but a dirt road alongside the river comes close to the site.

Graham Lodge on Tatla Lake.

The highway swings north away from the green Chilcotin River and farther along crosses one of its tributaries, Chilanko River, near the community of Redstone. Just past Chezacut Road is a fine modern restaurant named KiNiKiNiK on the Rafter 25 Ranch. Serving only organic food, it is almost completely self-sufficient. All the meats are from the ranch, humanely butchered in their nearby abattoir, and fruit and vegetables are all grown here or sourced locally. Check out their website, pasturetoplate.ca, for full details of their extensive enterprise. Plan on enjoying lunch here or even an overnight stay. There are a few elegant guest cabins on site

Confusingly, farther ahead there is another community named Redstone, also known as Tsideldel, a large Indigenous village on both sides of the highway with neat rows of houses along the hillside. You can stop here to stock up on fuel and other supplies. The large Indigenous graveyard, fenced off beside the highway and teetering at the edge of the slope above the river valley, is a reminder that hundreds of Indigenous people lost their lives to smallpox and other European diseases.

Chilanko Forks, the next community west, has no visible signs of settlement from the road but it is the official address for local

The store at Tatla Lake boasts an odd assortment of goods and services.

resorts. Puntzi Lake is the largest of several lakes and major fishing lodges are located here, including one, Woodlands Fishin (that's right, no "g") Resort, that has a restaurant and a bakery. Guests can fly in to Puntzi Mountajn Airport.

Chilanko Marsh, just north of the highway along the airport road, is one of a series of protected wildlife management areas in the Chilcotin, home to a variety of birds, as well as other wildlife, including beaver and mink. One of BC's Historic Places is nearby: Knoll House, a hand-hewn-log structure with a sod roof built around 1900 by Ole Nygaard, one of the Norwegian immigrants who settled at Hagensborg in the Bella Coola Valley in 1894. The ranch was later sold to Arthur Knoll who built an interesting two-storey, barn-like addition. The site is presently not open to the public.

For the next thirty kilometres or so the highway parallels the shore of long Tatla Lake, but it runs high above it and forests obscure any views. A good place for a break is the rest stop on Pollywog Lake, another protected area with adjacent marshes. Then the road comes down to the valley and turns sharp right and crosses a sweep of meadowland to the community of Tatla Lake, known for historic Graham Inn. It was built by Bob Graham, who arrived in the Chilcotin in 1891 and headed off to the Klondike gold rush, where he must have been successful. Upon his return ten years later, he bought an existing ranch at Tatla Lake, married, and started a family. In 1914, his wife Margaret opened the first post office and the village grew around them. His daughter Alexina was the first teacher at the new school; later, another daughter, Betty, opened a store.

In 1932, the Grahams decided to build a stopping place, a building so grand compared to most settlers' homes that it became known as Graham's Big House. It was the only place in the area that had electric light, produced from their own power plant, and running water. It had a large dining room with china and silver cutlery, handmade quilts in each of its six bedrooms—and a great reputation for good food and hospitality.

In the years that followed, the Big House became the Graham Inn and changed hands a couple of times. But it is still there on the waterfront, and still provides comfortable old-fashioned accommodation as well as food—and the only public bar in the area. There is a motel and a shop in the village, but the shop, West Chilcotin Trading Company, is more than the usual country store: it combines the post office with mechanical and tire repairs, and provides such services as tax and notary, as well as food. There is a good view across the lake toward the coastal mountains, and an even better one from the graveyard on the hill above the village.

The mural on the exterior of the store at Anahim Lake advertises their famous rodeo.

A bit farther along the road, a fine old log barn proclaims its geographical position. It's the Halfway Ranch, the midpoint between Bella Coola and Williams Lake. Everyone stops to take a photo here.

The settlement of Kleena Kleene is hard to find. Its centre seems to be the post office at a prominent corner of the road: an unmanned small log cabin with post boxes outside, used as the address for several ranches and guest lodges in the area. One Eye Lake, just up the road, has a handy forestry picnic area and then, as the forests close in, it's mostly an uninterrupted fifty-kilometre drive past Clearwater

ABOVE Sign outside the Anahim store.

OPPOSITE Tranquil Green River: the start of the climb to the pass.

Lake to the community of Nimpo Lake, named for the sprawling adjacent lake. The settlement is known as the Float Plane Capital of BC, a jumping-off point for fishing, hiking, and sightseeing trips in the remote mountains, and the community has a general store, a roadside inn and motel, and several restaurants. Popular guest lodges are sprinkled along the lakeshore.

From here on, the Chilcotin changes its face. In what is now known as West Chilcotin, the forests are thicker and the land climbs steadily through the foothills of the Coast Mountains to Anahim Lake, the last community before the great wilderness of Tweedsmuir Provincial Park and the road down to the coast.

Anahim Lake (not to be confused with the village of Anaham, much farther east) is the biggest settlement in the area (roughly fifteen hundred people) and has a small airport. It is the headquarters of the Ulkatcho Nation, once the centre of an extensive trading network and an important gathering place where families came together for potlatches and to hunt caribou, a communal job that entailed building drift fences and herding the animals into traps. In the Dakelh language, Ulkatcho means "fat of the land," for the area was rich with fish and game animals. Nearby is a rare source of obsidian, a glassy volcanic rock, once much in demand because of its ability to hold a sharp cutting edge for arrowheads and tools. It can be found on nearby Anahim Peak (Besbut'a), a pillared volcanic cone in the colourful Rainbow Range of the Coast Mountains. To learn more about this nation, see ulkatcho.ca. Nothing

Heckman Pass, at 1,521 metres on the divide between the plateau and the Bella Coola Valley.

much remains of the nearby old village but Alexis Creek is worth a stop, and not because it is the last community before the really adventurous part of this road begins. You must visit the hundred-year-old general store. Its exterior walls are painted with beautiful murals showing horses prancing against a background of snowy mountains, artwork that is not only excellently done but also very appropriate: the Alexis Creek stampede every July is authentic and one of the best.

The area is tainted by tales of the Chilcotin War, in which the Indigenous people took up arms to stop road surveyors and builders from constructing an alternative route to the Cariboo goldfields from the head of Bute Inlet to Alexandria on the Cariboo Road. Several of the colonial invaders were killed, troops were called in, the Indigenous ringleaders were hunted down, and five of them were later hanged for murder. These men, who had only been protecting their lands from outsiders, were posthumously exonerated. The whole event, one of many unfortunate clashes between colonial and Indigenous people, has been much investigated and argued over, but the Dakelh People won this war. The road was never built and they still have undisputed claims over a huge area of the land. A terse government stop of interest plaque near the Dean River Fishtrap Recreational Site tells the bare bones of this sad episode of the 1860s.

Beyond the village, the pavement ends and the road climbs steadily, crossing tranquil Green River and up into the subalpine meadows and mountains of Tweedsmuir Provincial Park, a totally different ecological zone. Even the air seems different here. It's worthwhile parking near Heckman Pass summit to walk around a bit and enjoy the peaceful subalpine environment and the flowers.

The summit is the divide between the Chilcotin Plateau and the Bella Coola Valley. And just beyond, the most adventurous part of this road begins. There is little advance warning. Highway 20, known here as the Heckman Pass Road, turns a corner and swoops suddenly down, heading southwest to a dizzying view of snowy mountain peaks. In less than forty-eight kilometres, it drops from the pass at 1,521 metres down to 363 metres in the balmy

An old cabin in the Bella Coola Valley.

coastal valley below—and not gradually. The steepest part of what is known as The Big Hill is ten kilometres of the narrowest switchbacks with road grades of up to 18 percent.

It's hard to imagine that before 1953 there was no road here at all, beyond a few dirt trails, no access from Bella Coola to the rest of the province except by boat or plane. Isolated by the mountain divide, the people on the coast pleaded for a government road, but to no available. So they took the matter into their own hands. Using bulldozers and shovels, a volunteer crew laboriously inched its way up the precipitous slope. A similar crew worked down from Alexis Creek. It took them a whole year, then they were free to come and go. The road is still known as the Freedom Road.

Once the road was finished, the government took on the maintenance and put up a few warning signs, but despite much improvement over the years it is still a road to be reckoned with. It is narrow, winding, and unpaved—and often closed because of heavy snow, landslides, or avalanches. It is described on the website dangerousroads.org (type "Heckman pass grades of up to 18 percent" in the search box) as "one of the most scenic drives in the country with grades of up to 18 percent, no guard rails and sheer drop-offs of many hundreds of feet" with "steep, brake-grinding switchbacks." The website also notes that it is such "a white knuckle gravel road that on occasion, tourists who have ventured down it have refused to return on it." But the locals take it for granted, and really its bark is far worse than its bite. Drive slowly and carefully in low gear and pull off for a rest and a photo op where you can. There is usually ample space to stop for a while beside some of the abrupt switchbacks.

Hagensborg Church.

When the road reaches the bottom of the hill and drivers can take their eyes off the road for a second, you will notice a complete change in the scenery: the valley of the Atnarko River is in the coastal rainforest—on the edge of the even thicker Great Bear Rainforest—with tall cedars hung with lichen, and a forest floor carpeted with ferns. This is still within Tweedsmuir Provincial Park, and the Atnarko Campground at the bottom of the hill is a popular tourist spot. The Atnarko is one of the great fishing rivers in the area, and it is also, when fish are spawning, one of the best places to see bears, both black and grizzly. There is a safe viewing platform on the river at Belarko, just before historic Tweedmuir Lodge near the Atnarko-Bella Coola River confluence. This famous old lodge runs guided tours and has a long list of things to do in the area, if you opt for further adventures and decide to stay on.

House of Numst' on Bella Coola's main street.

Farther along the Bella Coola Valley, visitors with an interest in geology will notice evidence of a great divide: the mountains of the Interior or Chilcotin Plateau north of the valley are rounded, made up of very old granite (formed between 15 million and 20 million years ago), which crumbles surprisingly easily, breaking up into long scree slopes of tumbled rock. To the south, the granite of the much younger Coast Mountains is still strong and shaped by glacial action into very sharp peaks. The divide is explained, once again, by the colliding of terranes and by the differential movement of Earth's tectonic plates, which, even now, are grinding inexorably, shifting the very land around us—fortunately in minute increments. There is a good explanation of all this on a story board in the rest area at the start of the Mackenzie/Grease Trailhead, where you will also find several other boards detailing the origin stories, crests, beliefs, and legends of the Nuxalk Nation, into whose territory the road now continues west. I was particularly interested to learn that the Nuxalk word for "human" is t'mista, meaning to dream, to aspire, to be aware, to be conscious.

Alexander Mackenzie, the first European to cross North America by land, came down to the valley here after his momentous journey across the Chilcotin Plateau in 1793. With help from Indigenous people along the way, he had followed for the most part the traditional and well-used Grease Trail that the Nuxalk and Ulkatcho people used as a trade route between the coast and interior of the province. They traded not only the oily eulachon fish that gave the trail its name, but also coastal greenstone and obsidian. When Mackenzie and his men stumbled into the village of Stuie, on Burnt Creek, they received such a warm welcome that he named the place Friendly Village. He was astonished to find one of his hosts wearing brass buttons. By the 1790s, trading had already begun between First Nations along the BC coast and early Spanish, English, and Americans who had stopped by in sailing ships, at first to search for the fabled Northwest Passage, then to trade for sea-otter furs.

Nuxalk people took the explorer and his men by canoe down river to the ocean at Dean Channel, where Mackenzie commemorated his arrival "from Canada by land" with an inscription, daubed in a mixture of bear's grease and vermilion (likely ground from red rock from the Rainbow Range) on a prominent slab, at what is now one of Canada's most historic places.

Starting at the Burnt Creek bridge, you can hike Mackenzie's route, a National Heritage Trail, all the way to the Fraser near Quesnel, a strenuous three-week, 450-kilometre trek. What an adventure road this would be! But a more family-friendly and far shorter excursion begins here too. It follows the first part of the trail, then loops around and returns, a five-kilometre hike that climbs two hundred metres to lookout points that provide a grand view of the mountain that Mackenzie named Stupendous.

Highway 20 continues west to the small community of Firvale, where Burnt Creek flows into the Bella Coola River, and farther along is the historic village of Hagensborg, which was established by Norwegian settlers in October 1894. Rev. Christian Saugstad and eight-four men arrived on the SS *Princess Louise* just outside the

OPPOSITE An old dock at Bella Coola.

Boats in the harbour.

mouth of the Bella Coola River. There was no wharf: the men and their supplies were taken to shore in Nuxalk canoes. The settlers had come from Minnesota (which had proved too cold and bleak) to stake out their government-allotted 160-acre homesteads on land quite similar to the fiord country of their homeland. The site of their settlement, about twenty kilometres up the Bella Coola River, had been chosen by Rev. Saugstad on a previous visit, and a rough trail along the river had already been bushed out.

The men, divided into construction groups of four, set to work to build small cabins before winter arrived, clearing the sites, cutting down the trees, and shaping the logs—an incredible amount of work. Five of the men soon quit and took the next boat south. But in spring another boat arrived with the remaining men's wives and children, and the settlement began to take shape. In this second year, the first Norwegian wedding took place in a newly built church, and soon there was a school and a post office. Some of the women had brought seeds with them. Home gardens were planted and flowers bloomed among the stumps. Not all the settlers became farmers: many chose fishing and logging. And in between times, all were kept busy constructing the first wharf at Bella Coola and a proper road up the valley.

Today Hagensborg has preserved much of its Norwegian heritage. There are several log homesteads in the area and right beside the highway, moved from its original location, is one of the settlers' original square log houses, furnished with pioneer artifacts. A story board outside outlines the settlement history. Nearby is the beautiful white United church which dates from 1910, a far grander building than the first humble version built in 1892 as the Augsburg Lutheran Church.

Before the highway reaches the townsite of Bella Coola, it passes the new Nuxalk community at Four-Mile (from the government wharf). This is Snxlh, or "sunny village," so named because it is in the part of the valley least shaded by the mountains. The community's administration office is here—your source of information for all the Nuxalk tours and events in the valley—and also the Acwsalcta, or "school of learning," where instruction is given in Nuxalk. Described as a three-dimensional work of art, this building is painted with the Nation's traditional emblems and has two great totems out front. One was made in 2002, the first to be raised here in thirty-five years; the other, carved from a six hundred-year-old cedar by artist Alvin Mack and his son Lyle, was erected in 2007 to celebrate the school's twentieth anniversary.

The first building of note as drivers pull into the townsite of Bella Coola, which today merges with the old Nuxalk village of Q'umk'uts, is the Kopas general store, founded in 1937. No longer a grocery store, today it sells just about everything else you could need, including maps, supplies for fishermen, hikers, and tourists, and also a huge selection of mementoes, including local books, and Nuxalk art and jewellery. In a way it has taken the place of the old HBC store that was built here in 1869.

Along the street is a white-painted United church and right beside it, the ancient House of Numst', or "house of stories," a replica of a traditional longhouse built of cedar planking and painted a dark red. Its brightly painted entrance pole tells the story of Nusmata, the legendary place of Nuxalk origin. Inside, two more totems support the roof. This intriguing building, a replica of a far older one, was constructed in 1968 by a group of young Nuxalk volunteers (most of whom are now Elders) who wanted a meeting place where their emerging cultural resurgence would be encouraged and flourish.

Now the House of Numst' is on the brink of a new life: It will be completely restored to become the headquarters for another active group of volunteers who run the community Nuxalk Radio and are leaders in the promotion and use of Nuxalk language and traditions. In the fall of 2021, after much fundraising, the building was dismantled and, the radio's website reads, "put into seclusion as part of the transformational process of restoration." The project is expected to take about a year.

Nearby is the Copper Sun Gallery of Nuxalk art, which is also the area tourist centre and runs many of the guided tours. One of the most appealing tours is a hike into the deep forest to see hidden petroglyphs thought to be thousands of years old. The Bella Coola Valley Museum in a log schoolhouse and surveyor's cabin up on the hillside on the way to the harbour should also be on your "must visit" list.

Highway 20 ends just past the active boat harbour and the BC Ferries dock (summer-only service to and from Port Hardy on Vancouver Island), and a few kilometres beyond is Clayton Falls, a great spot for a short hike and a beach picnic. Here, where Clayton Creek hurls pell-mell over glacially scoured rocks, BC Hydro built a run-of-river electricity generating station, a spawning channel for pink salmon, and a small day park. A trail leads up to a viewing platform overlooking the falls, and another leads out to the beach. Here you can watch the boat traffic, and the seals playing beside the creek confluence, and look far across the fiord to the historic Tallheo Cannery.

This is another of Bella Coola's historic treasures. Built in 1916, it was one of hundreds of canneries along the BC coast set up in the early twentieth century to process and ship salmon, and its workers and their families lived in the company village. The site is open for day tours, by boat from the harbour, and it also provides B&B accommodation in a comfortable 1920s guest house (bellacoolacannery.com). What a wonderful wilderness setting in which to end the long journey from Williams Lake, and to plan future trips into the Great Bear Rainforest: cruises to the Mackenzie Rock, hot springs, giant cedars, ancient petroglyphs, and organized excursions for hiking, fishing and bear and whale watching. Adventures unlimited...

OPPOSITE Clayton Falls.

RECOMMENDED READING

Akrigg, G.P.V., and Helen. B. Akrigg. *British Columbia Chronicle, 1847-1871: Gold and Colonists*. Vancouver, BC: Discovery Press, 1977.

Birchwater, Sage. *Chilcotin Chronicles*. Halfmoon Bay, BC: Caitlin Press, 2017.

Campbell, Colin. *Trails of the Southern Cariboo*. Calgary, AB: Rocky Mountain Books, 1998.

Cannings, Richard, and Cannings, Sydney. *The BC Roadside Naturalist*. Vancouver, BC: Greystone Books, 2002.

Coull, Cheryl. *A Traveller's Guide to Aboriginal BC*. Vancouver, BC: Whitecap Books, 1996

Downs, Barry. *Sacred Places: British Columbia's Early Churches*. Vancouver, BC: Douglas & McIntyre, 1980.

Elliott, Gordon R. *Barkerville, Quesnel and the Cariboo Gold Rush*. Vancouver, BC: Douglas & McIntyre, 1978.

Fowler, Julie. *The Grande Dames of the Cariboo*. Halfmoon Bay, BC, Caitlin Press, 2013.

Hill, Beth. *Sappers: The Royal Engineers in British Columbia*. Ganges, Horsdal & Schubert, 1987.

Hutchinson, Bruce. *The Fraser*. Toronto & Vancouver: Clarke, Irwin & Company Ltd, 1959.

Large, R.G. *Skeena: River of Destiny*. Vancouver, BC: Mitchell Press, 1957.

Lee, Norman. *Klondike Cattle Drive*. Vancouver, BC: Mitchell Press, 1960.

Ludditt, Fred W. *Barkerville Days*. Vancouver, BC: Mitchell Press, 1969.

Neering, Rosemary. *Continental Dash: The Russian-American Telegraph*. Ganges, BC: Horsdal & Schubart, 1989

Ormsby, Margaret. *British Columbia: A History*. Toronto: McMillan Company of Canada Ltd., 1958.

Patenaude, Branwen. *Trails to Gold*. Victoria, BC: Horsdal & Schubart, 1995.

Patenaude, Branwen. *Trails to Gold Volume 2: Roadhouses of the Cariboo*. Victoria, BC: Heritage House Publishing, 1996.

Paterson, T.W. *Ghost Towns & Mining Camps*. Langley, BC: Stagecoach Publishing, 1979.

Ronayne, Irene. *Beyond Garibaldi*. Lillooet, BC: Lillooet Publishers Ltd, 1971.

Rothenburger, Mel. *"We've Killed Johnny Ussher!"* Vancouver, BC: Mitchell Press, 1973.

Rothenburger, Mel. *The Wild McLeans*. Victoria, BC: Orca Books, 1993.

Skelton, Robin. *They Call it the Cariboo*. Victoria, BC: Sono Nis Press, 1980.

Stangoe, Irene. *Cariboo-Chilcotin: Pioneer Places and People*. Victoria, BC: Heritage House Publishing, 1994.

Veillette, John, and Gary White. *Early Indian Village Churches: Wooden Frontier Architecture in British Columbia*. Vancouver, BC: UBC Press, 1977.

Wade, Mark S. *The Cariboo Road*. Victoria, BC: The Haunted Bookshop, 1979.

Woolliams, Nina G. *Cattle Ranch: The Story of the Douglas Lake Cattle Company*. Vancouver, BC: Douglas & McIntyre, 1979.

INDEX

150 Mile House, 79, 88–89, 133
153 Mile House. *See* Mountain House

Alaska, 78–79, 121, 152, 160
Alexandria, 202
Alexis Creek, 196, 202–3
Alexis, Chief, 70
Alkali Creek, 71
Alkali Lake Ranch, 66, 72
Alkali Lake, 69, 72
Anaham (Tl'etinqox), 192, 196, 200
Anahim Lake, 199–200
Anahim Peak (Besbut'a), 200
Anderson Creek, 170
Anderson Lake, 91, 102–3, 107, 110
Anspayaxw (Kispiox), 159, 160
Antler Creek, 146
Apollo Lumber, 128
Ashcroft, 85, 89, 139
Atnarko Campground, 204
Atnarko River, 204
Augsburg Lutheran Church, 209

Bailey bridge, 146
Baker, Russ, 124
Barkerville, 57, 77, 85, 131–32, 121, 143–49
Beaver Creek, 140
Beaver Lake House, 140
Beaver Valley, 140

Beaver Valley Road, 140
Becher House, 191
Becher's Pond Recreation Site, 192
Becher's Prairie, 188
Begbie, Matthew Baillie, 113
Belarko, 204
Bella Coola, 9, 79, 185, 192, 196, 199, 203, 205–6, 208–10
Bella Coola River, 206, 208,
Bella Coola Valley, 198, 202–3, 205, 210
Bella Coola Valley Museum, 210
Bella Coola's Big Hill, 104
Bennett, W.A.C., 158
Bering Strait, 152, 160
Big Bar Creek, 66
Big Bar Guest Ranch, 66
Big Bar Lake, 68
Big Hill, 104, 203
Big Lake, 133, 139
Binche, 127–28
Black Point, 51
Bonaparte First Nations Reserve, 32
Bowron Lakes, 143, 148
Bralorne, 99, 102, 104
Bridge of the 23 Camels, 58, 60, 111
Bridge River, 91–2, 95, 98–99, 102–4
Bridge River Valley, 102
Bridge Street, 162
Brigade Hill, 169

Brigade Lake, 170–71
Brigade Trail, 172
British Royal Engineers, 132
Bryant, J.C., 140
Buckskin Ranch, 78
Bulkley Canyon, 151
Bulkley River, 151–54
Bull Canyon, 197
Bullion Mine, 140
Burnt Creek, 206
Bute Inlet, 202

Cache Creek, 25, 29, 34, 61, 111, 167, 178
California, 121, 131, 189
Cameron Ridge, 133, 141, 146–47
Campbell Creek Road, 173
Canadian Museum of History, 50
Canadian National Railway, 79, 106
Cariboo City, 146
Cariboo gold rush, 87
Cariboo hills, 132
Cariboo Lake, 133, 143, 146
Cariboo Mountains, 55, 141, 143
Cariboo Plateau, 27, 72
Cariboo River, 131, 144–45, 148
Cariboo Trail, 58, 106
Cariboo Wagon Road, 77, 79, 84, 132
Carpenter Lake, 91, 99, 102–3
Carr, Emily, 163–65
Carson, Robert, 62
Castle Rock Hoodoos Provincial Park, 27
Cayoosh 92, 106
Cayoosh Creek, 58, 91–92
Cedar City, 143,
Cedar Creek, 38
Cedar Point Provincial Park, 143
Chapperon Lake, 181
Charette, Pierre, 20
Charette Creek, 29
Chezacut Road, 197
Chiaro, Annie, 89
Chilanko Forks, 197
Chilanko River, 197
Chilcotin, 69, 191–92, 185, 196–98, 200
Chilcotin Country, 69, 185
Chilcotin Highway, 191

Chilcotin Plateau, 192, 203, 205–6
Chilcotin River, 75, 188, 190, 192, 196–97
Chilcotin Road, 79
Chilcotin War, 167, 202
Chillinetza, Chief, 178
Chilliwack, 178
Chimney Creek valley, 72
Chinatown, 145
Christ Church, 52
Church of Our Lady of Good Hope, 117, 124
Church of Our Lady of the Rosary, 153
Church of St. Kateri, 128–29
Church of St. Mary Magdalene, 154, 158
Church of the Holy Cross, 113, 115, 127–28
Church of the Immaculate Conception, 88
Church of the Sacred Heart of Jesus, 196
Churn Creek Bridge, 58, 73–74, 191
Churn Creek, 69, 73
Circle W Ranch, 26
Clayton Creek, 210
Clayton Falls, 210
Clinton, 73
Coast Mountains, 91, 185
Coldwell Ranch, 66
Coldwell, Henry, 63
Colin, Pierre, 70
Collins Overland Telegraph Line, 151, 160
Comet Creek, 147
Compton, Pym Nevins, 49
Coquihalla Highway, 173
Cornwall, Hugh, 89
Cottonwood House, 149
Cottonwood Marina, 127
Cottonwood Park, 123–24,
Cowan, Charles, 89
Cowan, Sonia, 89
Cowan, Vivien, 89
Canadian Pacific Railway (CPR), 169, 176, 181
Cranberry Junction, 42, 165
Cranberry River, 165
Crater Creek, (Lax Mihl), 39

INDEX **215**

Criss Creek, 20, 26
Crosina, Clara, 133
Crosina, Lillian, 136
Crosina, Louis, 133

Dakelh Nation (Carrier), 120-21, 123, 125, 127, 200, 202
Dancing Bill's Gulch, 141
Dawson City, 196
de Versepeuch, Comte, 70
Deadman Falls, 29, 32
Deadman River, 19-20, 26-27
Deadman Road, 29
Deadman Valley, 19, 29, 34
Deadman Valley Lakes, 34
Dean Channel, 206
Deep Creek (now Hawks Creek), 79, 139
Dewdney, Edgar, 156
Diamond S cattle ranch, 62
Doc English Bluff, 185
Dog Creek Dome, 70-71
Dog Creek Stage Lines, 70
Dog Creek Valley, 70
Douglas Lake Ranch, 181
Douglas Lake Road, 176-77
Douglas Lake, 169-70, 176-77, 180-81
Douglas Road, 122
Douglas, James, 113
Downing Provincial Park, 63
Dozier, Karl, 106
Dunlevy Ranch, 87
Dunlevy, Peter, 85, 140

Eagle, Charles, 88-89
Edge Hills, 63
Edith Lake, 170
Empire Valley, 73
English Bridge, 181
Esk'et, 72

Farwell Canyon, 75, 188, 190
Fidler, Peter, 167
First Avenue, 165
First World War, 34, 111
Firvale, 206
Fisherman's Road, 52

Fishery Bay, 49
Forest Service Road 8400, 146-47
Fort Alexandria, 27
Fort Berens, 60
Fort Chilcotin, 197
Fort Kamloops, 20, 27, 173. *See also* Kamloops
Fort Point, 52
Fort St. James, 117, 120-21, 128-29,
Fort Stager, 160-61
Four-Mile, 209
Fraser Plateau, 91
Fraser River, 57-58, 68-69, 73, 77, 87, 91-92, 112, 131, 185, 189
Fraser, Simon, 55, 92, 117, 120

Gang Ranch, 69, 73-44, 191
Ghost Lake, 144, 147
Gingolx (Kincolith), 48, 50-52,
Gingolx church, 50
Gingolx River, 52
Gitanmaax, 152
Gitanyow, 164-65
Gitlaxt'aamiks, 38, 42, 152, 165
Gitsegukla, 162
Gitwangak (Kitwanga), 162-63, 165
Gitwinksihlkw, 42, 43, 44, 49
Gitxsan ta'awdzep, 163
Gitxsan, 49, 151-54, 156, 158-59, 161-64
Glen Vowell (Sik-E-Dakh), 159
Gold Bridge, 102, 104
Golden River Dam, 143
Graham, Alexina, 198, 218
Graham, Betty, 198
Graham, Bob, 198
Graham, Margaret, 198
Grease Trail, 162, 164, 205-6
Great Bear Rainforest, 37, 185, 204, 210
Great Northern Railway, 79, 156
Green River, 200, 202
Green, Alfred, 49
Greenville, 49
Grinder, Phil, 63
Group of Seven, 89
Guichon, Joseph, 176

Hagensborg, 198, 206, 208
Hagensborg Church, 204
Hagwilget Canyon, 154, 156
Haida Gwaii, 163
Halfway Ranch, 199
Haller, Joseph, 58, 68
Hamilton Ranch, 140
Hance, Tom, 196
Hanceville, 192, 196
Hands of History, 153
Hare, Alex, 168-72
Harper, Jerome, 74
Harper, Thaddeus, 74
Harris, Walter, 160
Harrison Hot Springs, 115
Harrison Lake, 112, 115
Hawks Creek, 79, 139
Hazelton, 152-54, 156, 160, 162
Heckman Pass, 202-4,
Heckman Pass Road, 203
Heckman Pass summit, 203
Heritage Park, 110
Highline Road, 91, 103, 107, 110-11
Highway 1, 20, 25, 27, 29, 34,
Highway 5, 172-73, 176, 178
Highway 5A, 170, 173,
Highway 16, 42, 117, 121, 152-53, 156, 161, 163, 165
Highway 20, 72, 79, 203, 206, 210
Highway 24, 158
Highway 26, 127, 148-49
Highway 27, 121
Highway 37, 42, 162-65
Highway 62, 153-54
Highway 97, 61, 68, 77, 79, 87-88, 133, 149, 182, 185
Highway 99, 60, 91, 110-12
Highway 113, 37-38, 165
Highway 152, 37
Holy Trinity Church, 57, 61
Hope, 173
Horsefly (Harper's Camp), 74, 131, 136, 140, 143
Horsefly River, 140
House of Numst', 205, 209
Hudson's Bay brigade trails, 27, 170

Hudson's Bay Company (HBC), 28, 49, 60, 120, 123, 156, 173, 197, 209
Hunt, Henry, 165
Hunter, Joseph, 143
Hwistesmetxē'qen, 173

In-SHUCK-ch Forest Service Road, 113
Interior Plateau, 20, 177
Ishkheenickh River, 49

Jackson Road, 171-72
Jackson, A.Y., 89
Jesmond, 57, 63, 66
Johnson, Helen, 79
Johnson, Rudy, 78-79, 188
Johnston, Ingrid, 88
Johnston, Ty, 88
Joseph Road, 98
Junction Sheep Range Provincial Park, 189

Kamloops, 9, 19, 20, 27, 168-69, 170, 173, 178, 181, 182
Kamloops Lake, 20
Kamloops Road, 173, 177
Keatley Creek, 9, 19, 34, 168-70, 173, 176, 178, 182
Keithley Creek Road, 144-45
Keithley Creek, 131, 139, 143-44, 146
Kelly Lake, 63
Kelly, Edward, 63
Kelly, Jim, 169, 173
KiNiKiNiK on the Rafter 25 Ranch, 197
Kispiox (Anspayaxw), 159, 160
Kispiox River, 159-60
Kispiox Valley Road, 156, 158
Kitsumkalum Lake, 38
Kitwancool, 152, 164
Kitwanga, 160, 162-63
Kitwanga River, 162-64
Kitwanga River valley, 163
Kleena Kleene, 199
Klondike gold rush, 198
Knoll, Arthur, 198
Knoll House, 198
Knutsford, 170-71

'Ksan, 154, 156, 158
Kwah, Chief, 121, 124
Kyah Wiget, 153

Ladies Creek Recreation Site, 146
Lakeshore Drive, 127
Lakeshore Road, 124
Laurier, Wilfrid, 34
Lava Lake, 38-39
Lax Anhlo'o, 49
Laxgalts'ap, 49, 51-52
Lee, Norman, 192
Lee's Corner, 192, 196
Leeson, Mel, 50
Likely, 133, 136, 140, 143-47
Likely Road, 133, 136
Likely, John "Plato," 143
Lillooet, 57-58, 66, 91-92, 95, 99, 104, 107, 110-13, 133
Lillooet Lake, 106, 110, 112
Limestone Mountain, 140
Little Red Schoolhouse, 133
Long Lake, 168, 170-71
Long Lake Road, 170
Long Portage, 106, 110
Lowhee Creek, 146
Lynn, Billy, 85, 87
Lytton, 58

Mack, Alvin, 209
Mack, Lyle, 209
Mackenzie Avenue, 78
Mackenzie Rock, 210
Mackenzie, Alexander, 120, 167, 206
Manning Road, 171-72
Marble Canyon, 61
Marble Range, 63
Matthew River waterfalls, 147
Matthew River, 133, 147
McAbee Fossil Beds Heritage Site, 32
McKay, George, 50
McLean, Allan, 168, 170
Mclean, Angele, 170
McLean, Archie, 168-69, 178
Mclean Brothers, 167, 168, 170-71
McLean, Charlie, 168

McLean, Donald, 167
McLean, Sophia, 167
McLeod, John, 168-69, 171, 173
McNeil, Calvin, 50
Meadow Lake, 68
Medeek, 161-62
Meldrum Creek, 78, 188
Meldrum Creek Road, 188
Merritt, 9, 170, 173, 176
Mile "0," 58, 93
Mill Bay, 52
Miner, Bill, 181
Minto, 104
Mission Dam, 91, 98, 99
Mission Hill Road, 107
Mission Mountain, 102-3, 111
Moha, 99
Moore, John, 89
Moorhead Lake, 140
Morice, Adrien-Gabriel, 125, 153
Moricetown, 153
Mount Currie, 110, 112-13
Mount Pope, 128-29
Mountain House, 57, 63, 131, 133, 139

Nagwentled, or "place of landslides," 191
Nak'azdli, 117, 120
Napier Lake, 172-73
Nass, 37-38, 48-49
Nass estuary, 51
Nass River (K'alii-askim Lisims), 37, 41, 44, 162, 165
Nass Valley, 37-38, 41-42, 49
Nechako Valley, 121
Necosli River, 120
'Nekt, 163-65
Nemaiah Valley, 196
New Aiyansh. *See* Gitlaxt'aamiks
New Hazelton, 156
New Hazelton Visitor Centre, 153
New Westminster, 132, 160, 170, 178, 180-81
Nicola Barn, 178
Nicola Lake, 173
Nicola River, 170, 177, 180-81

Nicola Valley, 167, 176, 180
Nicola's Country, 167, 173
Nicola's River, 173
Nimpo Lake, 200
Nisga'a Nation, 37–42, 44–52
Nisga'a Highway, 42
North Bentinck Arm, 185
North West Company, 20, 120
Northwest Passage, 206
N'Quatqua (Port Anderson), 110
Nusmata, 209
Nuxalk Nation, 205

Odin, Frank, 84, 87
OK Ranch, 58, 68
Old Hazelton, 153, 156
Ole Nygaard, 198
Oliver Street, 78
Omineca gold rush, 152
One Eye Lake, 199
Onward House, 89
Onward Station, 89
Ottawa, 50
Our Lady of Good Hope, 117, 124–25

Pacific Great Eastern Railway, 79
Pacific Western Airlines, 124
Palmer, H. Spencer, 132
Palmer, William, 168–69
Paquette Lake, 145
Parker house, 139
Parker, William, 139
Pass Valley, 29
Patenaude family, 136
Pavilion, 20, 57, 60–61, 63, 66, 92
Pavilion Forest Road, 92
Pavilion Mountain, 61
Pear Lake, 63
Pemberton, 91, 110
Pierce Memorial United Church, 159
Pinchi (Binche), 127
Pinchi Creek, 128
Plaskett, Joe, 89
Polley Lake, 141
Pollywog Lake, 198
Pope, Franklin, 121

Porcupine Creek, 63
Port Douglas, 84, 112–13, 115
Port Hardy, 210
Prairiedale, 123
Prince George, 9
Prince Philip Point, 180
Prince Rupert, 48, 156
Princeton, 173
Pritchard Road, 139
Puddle Produce, 85, 87
Puntzi Lake, 198
Puntzi Mountain Airport, 198
Pyper, Robert, 87

Q'umk'uts, 209
Quesnel, 77, 79, 85, 88, 143, 149, 160, 206
Quesnel Lake, 131, 141
Quesnel River, 139
Quesnelle Forks, 137, 139, 143–45
Quilchena, 176–77, 180
Quilchena Hotel, 176

Rainbow Range, 200, 206
Rattlesnake Grade, 63
Rattlesnake Rocks, 29
Redstone (Tsideldel), 197
Reidemann Wildlife Sanctuary, 72
Reservoir Road, 74
Richfield, 143
River Trail, 55, 57, 63, 66, 68, 70–72
Robinson, Gerald, 50
Roche de Boule Mountains, 154
Rosette Lake Road, 144
Roxborough, William, 169
Royal BC Museum, 50, 163
Royal Engineers, 132, 144
Rudy Johnson Bridge, 188
Rush Lake, 181

Salmon Arm, 182
Salmon River, 181–82
San Jose River, 88–89
Sand Lake, 38
Saugstad, Christian, 206, 208
Savona, 20

Second World War, 28
Secwépemc, 20, 79, 88
Seeley Lake Provincial Park, 161
Seton Lake, 91, 102-3, 107, 110-11
Seton Lake Band, 107
Seton Lake Campsite, 111
Seton Lake Provincial Historic Park, 107
Seton Portage, 99, 102, 104, 107, 110
Seton River, 103
Shalalth, 104, 106-7
Sheep Creek Bridge, 188
Short Portage, 106
Shumway, 168, 170
Shumway, Amni, 168, 171, 173
Shumway Lake, 173
Shuswap, 26, 182
Shuswap Lake, 182
Simon Fraser University, 91
Skatin, 112-13
Skeena River ('Ksan), 37, 151-54, 158-59, 161-62, 164-65
Skeetchestn People, 20
Skookum Lake, 27
Skookumchuck, 112-13
Skulow Lake, 139
Smithers, 158
Snowshoe Plateau, 131-32, 143, 146
Snxlh ("sunny village"), 209
Soda Creek Road, 78-79
Soda Creek Townsite Road, 84
Soda Creek wharf, 139
Soda Creek-Macalister Road, 87
Soda Creek, 77-79, 84-85, 87, 139-40, 188
South Thompson River, 19
Spaxomin, 170, 173, 176-78
Split Rocks, 25, 29
Springfield Ranch, 79
Squamish, 110
ss *Charlotte*, 84, 87
ss *Enterprise*, 84
ss *Princess Louise*, 206
St. Nicholas at Spaxomin, 178
St. Andrew's Church, 51
St. Cecelia's Church, 129
St. Luke's Church, 182

St. Mary's Church, 20, 107
St. Paul's Church, 162
St. Peter's Anglican Church, 156
St. Theresa of the Child Jesus, 72
St'át'imc Nation, 92, 113
Stack Valley Road, 78
Stanley Park, 73
Stephens Jr., Albert, 50
Stewart-Cassiar Highway, 162
Stii Kyo Din (Rocher Déboule), 158
Stony Bay Road, 129
Stswecem'c Xgat'tem (Canoe Creek-Dog Creek First Nation), 62, 70, 73
Stuart Drive, 123
Stuart Lake, 117, 120, 123
Stuart River, 120, 123
Stuart, John, 120
Stuie, 206
Stum Lake Provincial Park, 196
Stump Lake, 169, 173
Sweeten, 113
Sxetl, 95

Tachie (Tache), 127, 129
Tachie Road, 128
Tallheo Cannery, 210
Tatkwa, Anna, 88
Tatla Lake, 197-98
Terrace, 38, 52
Terzaghi Dam, 102
Thompson, 19, 34
Thompson River, 19-20, 27, 62
Tl'azt'en Nation, 127, 129
Tod, John, 173
Tomlinson, Robert, 52
Toosie (Tl'esqoxt'in), 188
Trapp Lake, 173
Ts'kw'aylaxw First Nation, 61
Tse-kya (Hagwilget), 154, 158
Tseax Cone, 39
Tseax Peak, 42
Tseax River, 38-39
Tŝilhqot'in, 191
Tsimshian, 49, 160
Tweedsmuir Provincial Park, 200, 202, 204

Txemlax'amid, 161
Txseemsim, 49

Ulkatcho Nation, 200
United Church, 159, 209
Upper Bridge River, 102, 104
Ussher, John Tannatt, 168–69, 172

Valenzuela, Raphael, 70
Vancouver, 73-75, 110
Vancouver Island, 210
Vanderhoof, 117, 121
Vernon, 182
Victoria, 50, 55, 129, 140, 145, 164
Vidette Lake, 27–29

Wagon Road, 58, 60, 77, 132, 136, 139–40, 145
Walhachin, 19, 20, 26, 34
Wells Gray, 143
West Chilcotin Trading Company, 199
West Chilcotin, 200
Westwold, 182

Whiskey Creek, 78
Whiskey Flats, 148
Whitecap River, 107
Williams Creek, 143, 145
Williams Lake, 57, 70, 72, 78-79, 87-8, 185, 199, 210
Wolf Creek, 148
Woodlands Fishin, 198
Wright, G.B., 84–85

Xatśūll, 79, 84
Xaxl'ip (Fountain), 60
Xwísten, 82, 91–92, 95, 98

Yalakom River, 99
Yalakom Road, 66, 99
Yukon, 42, 162, 165, 196
Yunkws, Dan, 158

FOLLOWING SPREAD Golden Chilcotin landscape shrouded in autumn mists.

ABOUT THE AUTHOR

LIZ BRYAN is a journalist, author, photographer, and co-founder of *Western Living* magazine. Bryan has written several books, including *Pioneer Churches of Vancouver Island and the Salish Sea: An Explorer's Guide* (which was a finalist for the Lieutenant Governor's Historical Writing Competition), *Pioneer Churches along the Gold Rush Trail: An Explorer's Guide*, *River of Dreams: A Journey through Milk River Country*, and *Stone by Stone: Exploring Ancient Sites on the Canadian Plains*.